and hope
sure hope
you enjoy the
journey of these men &
women and the men the loved.

Angie Bowen

MW00444391

SAINTS
CODEPENDENT

GOOD FROM EVIL

Angie Galler Bowen

ISBN 978-1-64670-733-1 (Hardcover)
ISBN 978-1-64670-734-8 (Digital)

Covenant Books, Inc.
11661 Hwy 707
Murrells Inlet, SC 29576
www.covenantbooks.com

What do I really want? And, what is my spirit telling me is the best way to proceed?
—Oprah Winfrey, *O Magazine*, June 2003

We experience God to the extent that we love, forgive and focus on the good in ourselves and in others.
—Marianne Williamson, *Illuminata*

Faith, hope and love; the greatest of these is love.
—1 Corinthians 13:13

All experiences, no matter what, are gifts. They are a place of transformation, no matter how ugly that part of you journey might have been.
—Wayne Dyer, PhD, *I Can See Clearly Now*

Do One Thing Different.
—Bill O'Hanion

This book is dedicated to Dr. George Edgar Bowen, without whose support this book would never have been written. I would also like to thank Barnes & Noble of Knoxville, Tennessee, who graciously gave me comfortable overstuffed chairs and offered heavenly brews and confections while the majority of this book was written.

CHAPTER 1

The snow was coming down so hard that Libby couldn't see the road in front of her. New Year's Eve was unusually cold this year. Snow was a winter reality in Pisgah Forest, North Carolina, but this was one of the worst winters in years. The mountain road was treacherous as the snowplows hadn't come through yet.

"I have to make it to the hospital," Libby whispered to herself. "Please help me, God."

She was in labor. She was sure of it. Only a couple of hours before, her husband, Jerry, had punched her in the stomach. She was in her ninth month. The blow has brought her swiftly to the cold, beautifully tiled floor. Her water had broken. She lay there, in the fluid, unable to move. She waited until he, in a drunken stupor, had stumbled off to bed.

Then, when she was sure it was safe, Libby drew in her breath, pulled herself up, grabbed her car keys and made it ever so slowly to her car in the garage. She was determined to get to Transylvania County Hospital in time to save herself and her unborn daughter.

She would not go back. She would have her daughter and move forward. It was time. There had been enough, too much, violence. She had loved him. She had tried. It had been a hard year for her, but she had been in hell, for most of her life anyway.

Enduring Jerry's abuse had somehow been easier than the abuse she had endured from her father. At least it had seemed that way at first.

When she first met Jerry, he was kind and loving, and he had told her she was his "soul mate" because they had both grown up in abusive homes.

Just months after their wedding however, Jerry began to drink more and more and was angry most of the time. He had threatened her with his fists quite often and had actually used physical violence once before. She had become very afraid for herself and for her unborn daughter.

Libby was determined to begin again. She wanted more for herself; and oddly enough, Jerry's blow to her stomach, to their unborn child, had given her the confirmation she needed to move on.

She drove slowly, the pains getting worse by the moment. Thinking back over the past year, Libby remembered the good in Jerry. He really had been kind at first, genuinely interested in hearing her talk about the sexual abuse she had endured from her father. He drank more than she liked, but so did her father. That wasn't anything new to her.

They had talked for hours about their childhoods and the loneliness they both had felt as children. He only drank on the weekends and was more than decent to her when he wasn't drinking. He had a great job and was quite generous financially, and though she hadn't dated much, he treated her better than any man she had ever known. He was definitely the cutest. Even her father had said so.

She tried to understand Jerry's temper. He had externalized his depression into anger outbursts while she had internalized her own depression, hating herself and feeling ashamed.

"Not an uncommon pattern for males and females," per Libby's therapist, Helen.

Jerry told her how he had grown up in an abusive and extremely violent home when he was very young. He had lived in foster homes until he was a teenager, at which time he had run away and lived on the streets.

Jerry had promised Libby that he wasn't going to be like his father or his grandfather.

"I'm going to be different for my son," he had said and had patted her stomach lovingly.

Libby wanted that to be true. She had always tried to focus on the good in him. There was good. Libby believed there was good in everyone if you looked for it hard enough. Her Sunday school teachers had told her that for years. So had her mother, Norma.

The undertones of violence were always present, mostly in verbal abuse, which made Libby feel sad, unloved and unwanted. Most of the time Jerry would get angry and throw things or sometimes punch a hole in the wall, but he hadn't hit her until the day they found out she was carrying a daughter. And again today.

The level and severity of verbal abuse changed that first time he hit her. Jerry had wanted a boy so badly. It's all he ever talked about. Libby would just smile and say, "She might be a girl, you know." He would walk off and sulk, refusing to discuss the possibility.

She really didn't know the extent of his anger until they got home from the doctor's office that day. The doctor had told them Libby was carrying a girl. Jerry had been silent all the way home. As they walked into the garage, he picked up a baseball bat in the corner, one he had recently bought for his upcoming son. He had begun hitting his fist with it. Libby had been terrified. She had walked into the kitchen, put her purse on the counter, and tried to get behind the table as quickly as possible. But Jerry grabbed her arm, spun her around, and hit her hard behind her knees. She had crumpled to the floor, unable to move. Thank God she didn't miscarry.

That day, however, the day that he had hit her, changed her life forever. Even though the bat had been plastic, Libby hadn't been able to walk for several days and was surprised her bones weren't broken. Jerry didn't come home for a week. No one knew about the abuse because she was afraid of what Jerry might do if he ever found out that she told anyone.

His anger was escalating daily, and she had been afraid for a long time. She had already decided that she had to get out. She was slowly dying. Libby felt sorry for Jerry but realized, through her work with her therapist, that feeling sorry for someone is not necessarily loving them, certainly not the kind of feelings you base a marriage on.

That day, however, the day he actually hit her, she began to formulate her plan to leave him. *Why did it take him hitting her?* she often wondered. Abuse is abuse! She would wait until the baby was born, if at all possible; then, after they were discharged from the hospital, she would find a safer place to live. She would make it impossible to find her, not that he would want to try, but just in case.

Looking back, Libby whispered words of gratitude to God. She was beginning to see that a horrible stumbling block of violence had suddenly become the stepping-stone to her freedom. She finally dared to hope for the possibilities that still remained (something she'd heard from a PBS broadcast of Wayne Dyer), not just physical freedom but mental and emotional freedom as well.

Waves of nausea overcame Libby as she began to swerve in the road. The pain was awful, both from where Jerry had punched her in the stomach and from the labor pains.

She kept her hands on the steering wheel and willed herself to drive. She had taken the shortest route to the hospital, albeit the most treacherous. The back roads were steep and winding. Soon now. She could hear the snowplows on the main roads. Soon it would be safer to drive, and she would get there in time. Libby forced herself to think of the positives.

Even now, she felt sorry for Jerry. *Was that wrong*, she wondered, *to feel sorry for him?* Jerry's mother had died when he was a toddler, and his father had beaten him unmercifully, blaming him for his mother's death. Jerry had felt so alone and rejected, not to mention abandoned.

When he had been placed in foster care, he had been so hopeful. He was getting a real family! His foster father had sexually abused him and burned his flesh with his cigarette butts, and his foster mother threatened to send him back to the orphanage every time he made a mistake. She was sure that was why Jerry was so perfectionistic. He had needed for things to be perfect, from the towels being perfectly aligned in the bathrooms to the foods on his plate not touching each other. Helen surmised OCD (obsessive compulsive disorder), but "of course, I can't diagnose without seeing him," and Jerry would not go.

Libby could relate to Jerry's childhood though. Her own father had made her life a living hell with his emotional and sexual abuse, and her mother refused to acknowledge any of it. Libby had felt alone as well and had real trust issues with everyone, male and female.

Jerry's marriage proposal seemed like a gift from God. And she had truly loved him. At least she thought it was love. Thanks to a bibliotherapy assignment from Helen, a Christian therapist, she had come to realize that the kind of love she felt for Jerry was agape love, the kind of love she had been taught to feel for every human being. She had just wanted to help him, and herself, and marriage seemed the way to do it.

She felt empathy. From the very first time they talked about their childhoods, Libby had felt a strong connection with Jerry. She imagined it was because they had both survived abuse from the very people who were supposed to love and protect them.

Libby wanted to show Jerry the love that everyone deserved, God's agape love, given through mere mortals, the love that would surpass all human understanding.

She wanted that love from him as well. Libby had read somewhere that the best way to experience God, was to love, forgive, and focus on the good. It had been a book by Marianne Williamson called *Illuminata*.

She hoped, with all her heart, that they would be capable of that kind of love, knowing it would be hard for both of them, considering their backgrounds. Yet she was determined to try, and she offered him her love as unconditionally as she was capable of doing.

The winding road was icy in spots. She had another contraction, spun on the ice, and landed in a ditch. Freezing and terrified, she took the blanket she had grabbed on the way out and wrapped herself in it.

"I have to call for help," she murmured as she began searching for her phone.

She looked everywhere. It wasn't in her purse.

Jerry must have taken it, she thought. What would she do? What could she do?

Another contraction. They were coming closer together now.

Libby drifted in and out of sleep, thankful that she had grabbed the precious Native American woolen blanket, a gift from her mother last Christmas. She loved her mother. She had missed her these past months, but had understood how living with an alcoholic and abusive husband and having been raised by a stern and judgmental mother could change a person.

No matter what, she wanted a relationship with her. Libby again focused on all the good things her mother had done with her and for her throughout her life thus far. She was determined not to let the negatives gain a stronghold in her mind. The positives were too important to her, and she was thankful to focus on them.

Libby didn't condone her mother's behaviors, just understood them. She also loved her grandmother, albeit from a distance, as Libby was afraid of Grandmother more days than not. Again, she wondered if it was wrong to try and understand a person's behavior. To Libby, understanding had always been a necessary part of forgiveness.

Squeezing back the tears, Libby remembered her mother's warning: "Libby; he is all wrong for you. Please, honey, please don't marry him."

Norma had begged her daughter not to marry Jerry. Libby always thought it was because he had been drinking and, yes, a little too much, when she first met him. Norma wouldn't touch alcohol. She hated what it had done to Kenny, and she didn't want that kind of life for Libby.

But Libby had discovered she was pregnant a couple of months after she began dating Jerry. She didn't know whether it was her father's baby or Jerry's baby, as her father had wanted to give her a "proper good-bye" before her wedding. She had felt nine years old again, still unable to get away from him. She felt so ashamed, as her body withstood him and her mind went somewhere else once again. Libby shuddered as she remembered her father's strong, forceful behaviors when she tried to avoid him, begged him to leave her alone. He just said what he always said as he stroked her hair. "You will always be my little girl, Libby. I will always love you the most."

When she was younger, he was gentle, but as she became older, he had become more aggressive. She wondered if it was because she was beginning to avoid him as much as possible, spending the night with friends as often as she could.

She had, in fact, found out she was pregnant by stealing a home pregnancy test from a girlfriend's mother's medicine cabinet. She had been mortified at first. She thought for a fleeting moment about abortion, but she couldn't bring herself to take the life of an innocent baby. That would be murder for her convenience. Libby was scared but determined to let her baby live.

She knew she had to get out of her father's house though, and Jerry's proclamation of love and proposal of marriage seemed a perfect and timely path to take.

He had even seemed happy about the pregnancy. *I guess he thinks it's his*, she had thought, and Libby hoped it was. She had told him about her father's abuse as she wanted to be honest with her soon-to-be husband, not about the night before they married but all the childhood abuse.

Her father had almost pushed her into marrying Jerry, which Libby found strange. Looking back now, at the day they had met, her father and Jerry had seemed close, too close, like they had known each other for years.

Libby couldn't put her finger on it, just found it odd. As far as she knew, her father didn't know about Libby's pregnancy, just seemed to think Jerry hung the moon and he hardly even knew him.

Even now it startled her as she remembered Kenny touching Jerry's back almost intimately that afternoon. *My sick imagination,* she had thought and immediately dismissed it.

It had been romantic with Jerry, the way they stole away in the night to the justice of peace in Buncombe County. Kenny had met them there. She had been amazed that Jerry wanted to get married when she told him she was pregnant. She was almost eighteen when she told him. She could do whatever she wanted soon. And on her birthday, they eloped.

Her mother and grandmother had refused to witness their marriage, so why not just elope? At the time, it seemed the best thing to do. Why did her mother forbid her to see Jerry and yet her father pushed her toward him? She felt so confused.

Jerry was so good-looking, half black-half white, and had a beautiful permanent tan, which had all the girls hanging on him at that weekend barbeque, regardless of their race.

Grandmother detested him, of course, precisely because of his race; but Libby didn't care. Grandmother had chosen Kenny for Norma, and look how that had turned out!

Jerry had big chocolate eyes, light-brown skin, and dark curly hair. He was tall and lean and very friendly, almost too friendly. It was as if he had decided Libby was "the one." She wondered how it could be that he wanted her above all the really gorgeous girls that were throwing themselves at him. She decided she didn't care. She felt special for the first time in years.

Libby's home life had been cheery on the outside, yet dark and terrifying behind closed doors. No one knew, not even her best friend. Between her mother, who kowtowed to Grandmother like she was the queen of Sheba, and her alcoholic father, drunk more days than not, Libby felt her life couldn't get much worse.

Her life was consistently unpredictable. Her mother's moods depended on whether her own mother was pleased with her that week and whether or not Kenny had used her as his punching bag.

A tear rolled down Libby's cheek as she thought about her father's nightly visits. She was very young when Kenny started slipping into her bed. He was never violent. He always took her side when she and Norma had an argument. She was daddy's little girl and that was somehow supposed to make it okay, but Libby detested it.

She begged him not to do it. He was always gentle, and it had actually felt good physically, something she couldn't understand until in therapy.

It all made her feel so ashamed. How could she feel good physically from something that was so wrong? She hated him for it and hated herself as well. He had told her it was their secret, that Mom wouldn't understand and would hate Libby "because Daddy loves you the most."

Libby tried to tell her mother once. Her mother yelled at her before she could even finish her sentence, refusing to acknowledge her at all. She had simply screamed, "Libby, take the garbage out right now. It is falling all over the place."

Libby had done just that and had never mentioned it again. Often Libby thought about it though and wondered, *Why would she yell at me like that? Change the subject, then act like I hadn't said anything?*

It's like she knew what Libby was going to say and couldn't bear to hear it. Just recently, Libby's therapist, Helen, had explained to Libby that this kind of reaction was not uncommon, rather a form of unconscious repression and displacement of anger because the reality of what was happening to her little girl was too traumatic for Norma's psyche to accept yet.

"Repression is a protective mechanism, Libby, not a conscious choice," Helen had told her. "It doesn't condone her behavior; it does give you some insight into why it occurred." Helen had also said, "You did plant the seed of truth, though, Libby. And one day it will be watered."

The hope of that being true had sufficed. Libby had consciously chosen to focus on the good in her mother, just like Christ would have wanted for her, or so she believed as a frightened child and then a teenager. And her mother really was a good person.

Libby actually liked her mother, outside of her inability to protect her. Norma was so involved in Libby's life. She was the assistant campfire girl's leader and an assistant Girl Scout leader when Libby moved up to the next age group. She was the first to offer her help when Libby needed something, the first to volunteer for field trips at school, always out there helping Libby sell whatever fundraiser that came down the pike, holding her gently when Libby fell off her skateboard and skinned her knees, lugging her snowman into the garage when it started to melt because Libby couldn't bear to see him go away.

Libby fondly remembered her mother letting her have a male and female hamster so they could have babies. They added a new section of tunnels every time she earned her allowance. When the male, Buster, somehow got out of his cage (probably because the door was left open), Norma had no problem in cutting up the whole bottom lining of the couch when they heard him scurrying around in there.

They took long walks together, Libby stuffing bugs into her deep pockets along the way. Her mom read to her constantly, sometimes the same story over and over again. Once, she jumped into their community pool, with all her clothes on, when Libby got pushed in by a neighbor girl. Libby knew how to swim, but she had panicked, until her mom's arms were tightly around her, pulling her to the edge. Her mom used to ride down the slide with Libby, even though Norma could barely fit in the circular tubing. So many fun memories. Libby chose to focus on them now, as those memories were and always would be in Libby's heart.

Lying there in the dark, shivering under the woolen blanket, Libby braced herself against the steering wheel as another contraction hit her hard.

"Breathe, Libby, breathe," she repeated to herself over and over again.

Memories of her father kept creeping in. Libby indeed was afraid that her mother would blame her, if she had believed her. She would hate her. Her father had told her so.

"We can't have your mommy knowing about this," he had whispered in the dark. "She would send you away for sure."

That fear had continued to keep Libby quiet all these years, even the night before her wedding. A wave of nausea and guilt swept over her. Then she remembered a session with Helen in which they discussed the theory of learned helplessness. Libby had tearfully nodded her head in agreement.

"Yes, I did feel helpless that night and helpless all those years. It was like I had been knocked down so many times I couldn't get back up. Most days I didn't want to. I just wanted to die."

So when Jerry came along, Libby fell for his charms and decided he would be her knight in shining armor. Helen had helped Libby put her feelings for Jerry into perspective very early in their work together.

Libby had told Helen about the strong attraction she and Jerry had felt for each other right from the beginning. She explained to Helen how she thought she had finally been "rescued" when she fell in love with him.

Helen had stated quietly, "Libby, we fall into a hole. We choose to love."

Libby was amazed at the insights she had gained since working with Helen. She knew why she had chosen to love Jerry. She was so thankful for Helen and their work together.

She remembered her first session. Stepping into the waiting room at Helen's office was one of the hardest things Libby had ever done. Seeing a therapist was something Libby had been taught belongs to the crazies of this world. Libby had finally decided she was not crazy, more courageous than anything.

It wasn't normal to be crying all the time, wishing she was dead more times than not, and Helen had indeed helped her. She was beginning to learn who she really was in all of her life's drama, and it sure felt good to be "exploring what she wanted out of this journey she called life." (Helen had quoted an article from Oprah Winfrey that session.)

Helen often gave Libby bibliotherapy assignments, and Libby became so impressed with what she was learning through reading books and other resources. Oprah's *O Magazine* had quickly become a favorite, and she had gotten a subscription soon after that assignment. Unbeknownst to Oprah Winfrey, she was one of Libby's strongest mentors, along with Marianne Williamson and Wayne Dyer.

"It is a journey, Libby, a whole book of life, so to speak. And your life has many chapters," Helen had reminded her.

Thinking about that had made her life tolerable.

"This too is just a chapter," Libby reminded herself over and over again. "I will one day turn the page."

Libby had told Helen about Grandmother and how she had always been a little afraid of her. Grandmother was very strict and had always been extremely prejudiced. Libby could never understand why she was supposed to steer clear when it came to choosing friends from another race. She admitted, however, that there was a part of her that admired her grandmother greatly.

Grandmother had refused to put grandfather into a nursing home when he was diagnosed with dementia. Grandfather had been an alcoholic for many years but had given it up completely when Norma was a teenager.

His neurologist told them that the heavy binging had taken its toll however. Because of the heavy drinking and playing football for many years (even into semipro), he had irreversible brain atrophy, which eventually progressed to the point where Grandfather couldn't do anything by himself. Grandmother truly did love Grandfather Hugo. She would tell the funniest stories about how they had met and he had "won my affections."

Even though all her socialite friends, even his own blood, advised her to "put him away," Grandmother wouldn't hear of it. There were aides and nurses who helped; but Grandmother rarely left Grandfather's side, only to attend monthly charity board meetings and, of course, her weekly penny poker group, something she looked so forward to each Friday. She wouldn't allow any of the CNAs to wipe Grandfather after a bowel movement because "he needed to maintain some level of dignity." Libby knew it was taking its toll, yet Grandmother was adamant about helping him with that particular activity of daily living.

She read to him, just as she had to Norma and Libby, and brought him liquids and changed his adult diapers with such tenderness. Libby admired Grandmother's dedication to her grandfather.

Libby wondered, even now that she was in therapy, if her grandmother's dedication to Grandfather had been codependency. She saw it as love.

Her life did revolve around him for years and especially at the end. She had given up so much for him. After all, she was a pillar of the community, or so everyone had said. According to Libby's mother, Grandmother never criticized Grandfather's drinking.

She did, however, stay away from him when he would go on his binges. It was during that time that she became so active within the community. She took something bad and let God bring good from it. Libby admired that character trait in her grandmother. Libby learned that piece of information from Maria, the housekeeper, who had been with her grandmother and her mother and Libby for years. She was still with Grandmother, getting up in years herself, but Grandmother would never let her go. Instead, she had hired a cleaning crew to come in monthly for heavy cleaning and delegated Maria to mostly kitchen duty.

Maria had become like a member of their own family, as had her children. Libby found it ironic because Maria was Hispanic! Norma's rejection of Jerry stemmed from the fact that he had been drinking when Norma met him. With Grandmother, however, it was because Jerry was a Negro and "that just wouldn't do in our family."

Libby realized that both her mother and grandmother had good reasons (in their minds) for not liking Jerry.

"People must deal with the own demons, Libby," Helen had said. "Your mother is likely being an adult child of an alcoholic, even though he wasn't abusive before he became sober. Then she married an abusive alcoholic. Your grandmother's intense need to be accepted by her community. Status is her demon."

Norma had never gone against her mother's wishes. She had married Kenny because he had been handpicked by Grandmother. Libby often wondered what Constance held over Norma's head. What made Norma such a puppet, whose strings her grandmother pulled daily? If Grandmother wanted it, Norma did it, no questions asked, even if it was clearly not what Norma wanted.

Libby believed her mother was definitely codependent but couldn't pin down exactly why as the experts had explained the term in slightly different ways. Libby had read many self-help books. They were helpful and confusing. Helen had advised Libby to "take what works for you and leave the rest. Every word isn't meant for every reader."

She thought back to a day when she had heard Norma and Constance arguing about her mommy's wish to divorce her daddy. Libby was small then. But she remembered the argument now as if it were yesterday.

Grandmother had told Norma in no uncertain terms that she "will not get a divorce. You have a child to consider, and you will not disgrace this family! We can't forget that night with the priest now, can we?"

Libby hadn't understood what that meant, still didn't. She had thought of it a time or two over the years but was afraid to bring it up. The comment had made her mother's face turn white and had caused her to literally wither in her chair. Libby never even let her mother know she had overheard her and Grandmother all those years ago.

Norma had changed that day though. She agreed to stay married to Kenny. She hardly smiled anymore. Libby had heard her crying softly into her pillow on more nights than she could remember.

Grandmother was very rich. So was Kenny, but not as rich as Libby's grandmother. He came from a well-respected family though and made a "nice addition to our family." That was all that mattered. Kenny's father was a well-known attorney in Asheville when Norma met him. Kenny worked in the firm, one of the most sought after in the entire region. Grandmother insisted on a huge wedding when Norma and Kenny had married. Libby knew Norma would not approve of her marriage to Jerry, so they decided to elope. She didn't want to hurt her mother or grandmother.

Jerry told her father, and he called it "our little secret," just as he had done all those nights in her bed. She felt sick just remembering his smile as he said it. Libby hated her father yet hated herself for hating him.

Until she worked through some of those issues with Helen, Libby was suicidal more days than not. She now understood the normalcy of hating the behavior and separating the behavior from the person.

When Libby had married Jerry, her mother refused to visit her. She cut off all contact. So had Grandmother. The ultimate of abandonment and rejection. It had devastated Libby and had actually brought her and Jerry closer together. They were both glad they had each other to talk to.

Kenny had met them at the justice of the peace. He had seemed excited about "giving" her to Jerry, saying it over and over again. Libby couldn't put her finger on it, but her father kept making jokes about coming to visit his "little girl," and it made her feel queasy—then as well as now.

It had made Jerry angry though. Libby could tell by the way his jaw clenched when Kenny had said it. She remembered thinking, *Jerry loves me. He will take care of me and protect me from this monster.*

He would be depressed for days; then he would act like he was on top of the world, spending money lavishly, sleeping with anyone that said yes, male or female. Libby was grateful for the generosity, but his promiscuity terrified her. He had already given her more than one venereal disease.

Early on, Libby wished she could tell her mother or Grandmother about her life, especially that she was pregnant. An abortion would probably have been the option that Grandmother would have approved. That way her reputation and pride would remain intact. Libby couldn't even consider it, and she liked to think her mother would have approved of her choice to keep her unborn child.

Even if the child was her father's, she couldn't kill it just because of the way it was conceived. Libby had willed herself to see the baby as Jerry's and believed he would love him or her as much as she would. She believed he wanted to keep their child safe from harm, just as she did.

"Oh, God," Libby moaned. "Please don't let us die." Libby was crying now, sobbing into the blanket she kept wrapped around her. It was dark, no streetlights on Williamson Creek, and the temperature had dropped again. It was very cold, and Libby could see ice crystals forming on the trees around her. She didn't know how much longer she could last without turning on the heater, but she didn't want to risk any carbon monoxide fumes harming her or the baby, so she would wait just a little longer.

Libby continued to think back on the last few months of her life. It was the only thing keeping her sane at this point. She had known for some time that Jerry was cheating on her. She found hotel receipts and had even found used condoms in his pocket. It was so disgusting, like he was hoping she would find them.

"Either that or he didn't want to leave any DNA at the scene of the crime," she murmured to herself. "Libby, you have watched too many *Law and Order: SUVs*." She laughed out loud.

She did confront Jerry when she found the first condom. It didn't go well. She winced, even now, remembering how he made a fist toward her and hit the wall instead.

"I don't bother you anymore, do I?" he had said. "You should be thanking me."

He had become increasingly verbally abusive and threw things at her at least twice a week. She remembered his throwing her favorite teapot, one Grandmother had given her for her hope chest.

It had shattered on the tile floor. Libby had been terrified that Jerry would one day hit her, so she stopped mentioning the affairs or anything else that might set his temper off.

She did thank God that he was not expecting her to be sexually intimate with him at that point.

"No more STDs," she had muttered to herself.

It had stopped a few months after the wedding, one night when he had been extremely rough with her. He seemed to realize it because he had gotten up and told her, "We won't do this anymore. I won't hurt my little boy."

Libby's contractions were harder and coming faster. She remembered the breathing exercises she had learned at her Lamaze class, one that she had attended alone as Jerry had refused to go with her.

"That's women's stuff," he had said.

Libby had been grateful that her best friend, Carly, had gone to several classes with her.

If she had her phone, Carly would have been the first person she called. She was such a wonderful friend. They had been friends since childhood. It was at Carly's house that Libby had found the pregnancy test and used it. She wished now that she had told Carly about her life.

Carly had begun to pull away the last couple of months however. She had asked on more than one occasion for Libby and Jerry to join her and her husband for dinner and cards. Jerry would hear nothing of it. He wasn't social at all, unless it was with someone from his recovery group.

Another contraction. It wouldn't be long now. She had to be brave. Soon she would turn on the heater. She had already turned on the flashing emergency lights. Hopefully, someone would see them and get them to the hospital in time.

"Holy Spirit protect us," Libby whispered in the dark.

Thinking back to the first phone call from her mother after Libby's elopement made Libby smile. She had called right out of the blue just a few weeks after, and she wanted to see Libby. She was full of regret about not seeing her for so long. She wanted to make a fresh start and was willing to risk Grandmother's wrath to do it.

"Let's talk, my dear sweet daughter. Let's see if we can somehow begin again."

They had begun seeing each other at Quotations, an upscale coffee shop in Brevard, the cute tourist town outside of Pisgah Forest.

It was out of the way for Norma, who lived in Cashiers, but she wanted to be discreet.

She promised they would go and tell Libby's grandmother together when the time was right after the baby was born. Norma was hoping the three of them would present a united and irresistible front to Grandmother.

Their meetings had been so enjoyable, precious time for both Libby and Norma.

Last week Norma had told Libby, "I want to come to your house. It is time, Libby. We'll talk there, okay?"

Libby had readily agreed. That was today, and it had been wonderful seeing her mom again. At first they talked about insignificant people and things. "Surface talk," Libby's therapist would have called it.

People engage in surface talk when they are uncomfortable going any deeper. It is a way to have a relationship, yet remain emotionally safe, until they are ready to pursue the next level.

Her mother took a sip of her tea, breathed out slowly, and spoke. "Libby, I know I have made a lot of mistakes with you. I know that I am an imperfect human being and will make new ones, but I want to make amends for the ones I have already made."

She told Libby about her Al-Anon classes and the need to make amends was part of her healing process. For an instant, Libby had been incensed.

"Make amends? It's all about her," she muttered under her breath. "The apology is not for me. It is for her."

Angry that the apology was just her mother's need to complete the ninth step in her recovery process, Libby had almost asked her to leave. Tears had formed in her eyes, and she had wondered if it was a mistake reconnecting with Norma.

But it was like the Holy Spirit took over. Libby remembered something Helen, her therapist, had said.

"It is a giant step towards reconciliation when a person can apologize, regardless of the underlying motive(s)."

The LCSW had taken Libby's hands and whispered softly, "God knows the hearts of man, Libby, male and female. We are not privy to another's innermost thoughts and feelings, and there is a reason for that. Are you ready to step aside and let God be God? It can be a real relief to trust that God will bring good from all evil, Libby. Are you ready to let Him?"

It then occurred to Libby that her mother didn't know how what she had said was affecting Libby. How could she? Helen was right. We can't read each other's minds. She agreed it wasn't up to her to judge the reasons for the apology, just up to her whether to accept it or not.

She also realized that this wasn't just an apology. *She wants to have a relationship with me and my daughter and that's what I want also.* Libby had bitten her tongue, and her mother had continued.

"Libby, we have a chance for a new beginning, and that means I have to admit the truth about myself. I know I can be judgmental and selfish, just like my mother before me, protecting myself and my own reputation in the community. I lived in a constant state of anxiety. I wonder where I got that from." She laughed.

Her mother was indeed a social butterfly and a busy volunteer like Grandmother. She had even started volunteering at Transylvania Hospital on the day she had lunch with Libby.

"I would love to say my bad behavior stops today, but we both know it won't work. We will both make mistakes. I do think I am becoming less and less anxious now that I'm in recovery and seeing Helen. And I'm hoping that will help me to be a better woman and a fantastic nana!"

About that time they heard Jerry's Mercedes in the driveway. Libby was usually at Lamaze class that time of day. She had cancelled it because it was the only day her mother could come to her home.

"It's four o'clock. Why isn't he at work?" Libby asked as she stood up and walked to the window. He had parked out front in his new convertible.

The top was down, and he was kissing a woman in the seat beside him. The woman was wearing the diamond necklace Jerry had given Libby for Christmas. The one for which he had recently filed an insurance claim.

Libby was surprised that seeing Jerry with another woman meant very little to her. She was sad, yet not angry. She didn't even feel angry about the necklace, just thought, *Oh, that's where it went.*

Jerry looked up and saw Norma's car at the side of the house. He started his own car and left as fast as he could, the stranger's red hair blowing in the wind. Libby could see she was only wearing a robe. She looked like the woman who worked at their community copy center.

"Jerry was with another woman. She was not a business associate," Libby had informed her mother.

Norma spoke softly. She and Kenny had seen Jerry out with other women before, and Kenny had always made light of it, saying, "The man has a stressful job. He's just letting off steam, Norma. It's Libby he loves, just like I love you." He had smiled and kissed her.

Norma hated it, but what could she do? She had abandoned her own daughter. She wished she could tell her, but would Libby even believe her? Norma doubted it.

"I prayed for you, Libby. I knew that in time, it would come to light. Evil always does."

Libby answered softly, "Thank you for praying for me, Mama. Truth is, I probably wouldn't have believed you."

She couldn't believe the irony of it all. Norma was afraid she wouldn't believe her, and Norma hadn't believed Libby when she had reached out to her all those years ago about the abuse she was suffering from her father.

Libby wiped away a tear and told her mother, "Oddly enough, I feel very little. I am so sad for what could have been with Jerry but grateful for what will be between you and me. Let's focus on the positives, okay?"

They hugged each other and cried together for what seemed like an eternity. Libby told her mother about her mockery of a marriage. She told her that she had been pregnant before they married. She told her that it seemed like the right thing to do for her and her child.

Sobbing violently now, Libby told her mother about Kenny's nightly visits that had been going on since Libby was nine years old. She told her that she wanted to tell her and her grandmother but couldn't risk being sent away, as Kenny had threatened, if she told anyone.

"I did try to tell you once. Why did I even bother? You didn't believe me! You stopped me in mid-sentence, like you knew what I was going to say and just changed the subject to something about taking out the trash. Well, I felt like trash, Mama. Why couldn't I come to you for support?" she yelled at her mother. "I needed you," she sobbed. "I needed you."

Norma was quiet. She knew Libby needed to get it all out.

"I believed you would disown me," Libby cried. "That's what Daddy told me." Then she laughed hysterically. "And, ironically, that is exactly what you did anyway when I married Jerry. I needed you so much, and you were not there for me. I needed you!" She wept in her mother's arms, angry, yet so very thankful that her mom's arms were around her.

She calmed down after that, no longer angry, just grateful. Such a gift. She had waited so long for her mama's hug. She had a genuine hug, not a pat on the back, barely touching. Her mom had always been a hugger.

"Everything you have said is true, Libby," Norma said. "I was not there for you. I am so sorry. I wish I had been all those years ago when I lived in constant fear of my mother and of your father. I am not offering excuses. There are none. My behavior is abhorrent, and yet I feel helpless. I actually have felt helpless most of my life." Norma was wiping away her own tears. "I am hoping that you can find it in your heart to understand how afraid I was always on guard, fearing that I would be disowned. Maybe you can open your heart to one day forgive me?"

Libby smiled at her. "I already have, Mama. I already have. It is ironic to think about it now. But what you were experiencing, afraid that you would abandon me, at the same time that you were equally afraid Grandmother would abandon you."

Realizing they had been struggling with very similar issues, they hugged again. Libby held her back, feeling a pressure she hadn't felt before.

Norma rubber her daughter's back lovingly. "Looks like it's me and you, kid, and this baby." She patted Libby's stomach lovingly. "We will be okay. Do you hear me in there, little girl? This is your nana talking."

Libby smiled and looked at her mother. "Mom, what if Grandmother does disown you? What will you do? Dad would not be pleased. I always wondered if it was her money that attracted him to you. I don't mean that in a negative way. It's just that he has treated you so badly." Libby had always hoped her mom would divorce her father, but she never did.

Libby was thinking about the "night with the priest" comment her grandmother had made and wanted to ask about it so badly, but again bit her tongue. The time was not right. Her therapist, Helen, had taught her to "follow the Spirit's promptings."

Libby knew that whatever her grandmother held over her mother's head was profound. Norma had cowered to her mother as long as Libby could remember. She had watched her grandmother belittle Norma for years.

Nothing Norma did was right. She was always wearing the wrong outfit or gained too much weight or prepared a meal incorrectly, but Libby didn't understand emotional abuse until she began seeing Helen and gained insight into the devastating effect it was having on her own life.

"No more lies, Libby," Norma said and put her coat on. "I have to leave, but you and your daughter and I are going to begin again very soon. We, you and I together, are going to create a safe and loving environment for this little one." She touched Libby's stomach again and got her car keys.

Libby hugged her mother again. Just the feel of her arms around her, Libby had missed it so much. "Oh, Mama, thanks for not giving up on me."

Norma signed and said, "Honey, I never gave up on you. I gave up on me. I thought I couldn't break away, but I can. I am stronger now, and I am leaving your father. We will talk about it another time, but I need to get home now. Looks like the snow is beginning to lay. You know how I hate to drive in the snow since your schoolteacher had that awful wreck."

Libby walked her to the door. It had been a good visit. Norma had shared her experience at her Codependents Anonymous meetings and her Al-Anon meetings, and Libby had shared her experience seeing her therapist, which ironically was the same licensed clinical social worker that Norma had recently begun seeing as well. Libby like the fact that Helen was a family therapist, seeing family members together and/or separately. Helen believed that it was ultimately better for her clients, and it certainly had been for Libby and Norma.

Who would have known? she thought as she cleared the teacups away. Helen had certainly adhered to the HIPPA Law, the one that prevented her from sharing information about who she saw in therapy without informed consent. As she loaded the dishwasher, she wondered, *Maybe one day Helen will see the two of us together in one of those conjoint sessions she had originally wanted Jerry to attend with me.* She would ask at her next session.

She felt sad remembering again Jerry's response when she had asked him to see Helen with her.

"There's nothing wrong with me. You're the one who's crazy, crying all the time when I give you everything you want. You see her if you have to, but leave me out of it." He had been adamant.

Libby did cry a lot. Jerry accused her of being histrionic, but in reality, her therapist had told her she was struggling with clinical depression and that it was good to let herself cry when she needed to. "It's God way of helping you to cope, and it actually cleans away toxins from your body."

Helen had been a Godsend for Libby. In addition to being a LCSW, she had a specialty certification in cognitive behavioral therapy. She had asked Libby to talk to her doctor about starting an antidepressant, and the medication had helped Libby to focus more clearly. It had helped her to engage more thoroughly in therapy and at country club luncheons, one of the few places Jerry would let her go. He was really possessive of how she spent her time yet seemed totally uninterested in her. She wanted to understand his obsessiveness about her but couldn't. She and Helen had processed Libby's confusion about it all. Helen was very careful to never give Libby advice. Rather, she presented options, as she called them. The best options were ones that Libby was already aware of somewhere deep down inside. But she needed someone like Helen to help her sort them out.

Helen explained it as parts of her (and Jerry) battling with sometimes very conflicting needs.

"Hurting others is an inappropriate way to try and get legitimate needs met. Jerry isn't happy either, Libby. People don't stay angry all the time when life is at its optimum and one's innermost needs are being met. Neither of you are happy."

Helen had helped her to explore the possibility that she had been enabling Jerry to continue cheating on her and to continue the emotional physical and verbal abuse. Libby had become angry at first.

"I didn't cause him to drink. I certainly didn't make him have affairs! I confronted him once about his cheating and almost got his fist in my face."

"Of course, you didn't, Libby. You are not the reason for Jerry's abuse. You are simply the nearest target. Do you think it might be possible that by continuing to stay his nearest target may come across to Jerry as permission to continue the abuse?"

Wow, that really hit a nerve but Libby knew that Norma was right.

"One option might be to talk with him about the marriage and ask him if he is happy. And, of course, you do have your emergency bag hidden somewhere safe, right?" Helen always reminded Libby to keep an extra set of clothes, car keys, and extra cash hidden in a bag where Jerry couldn't find it, just in case.

Libby remembered her mother saying approximately the same things about Al-Anon. She had said she resented going at first because some of the women there actually blamed themselves and had begun to think they were the cause of their husband's drinking and drugging and cheating. Many of them came once and never came back.

When they had learned about enabling, many of them blamed themselves for all the problems in their marriages. But Norma never did accept that blame. As she put it, "I told them that I may have enabled him to continue his abuse of me by staying with him and trying to love him, but I didn't cause him to be a drunk. And I didn't cause him to be abusive in the first place. He made that choice all on his own." Norma was passionate about that. She told the group in no uncertain terms. "I am here to tell you that we are not the reason they are sick. And we aren't sick for loving them. We are saints for loving them! We became sick for continuing to allow them to abuse us after the very first incident of abuse. It took a while to finally say enough is enough, but we're here now, aren't we, ladies? And some of our spouses are over there really trying to put their lives back together." She had pointed to the building next door to theirs.

Norma had laughed as she shared this memory with Libby. She said the women around the table all stood up and clapped, and the whole tone of the meetings changed after that. Some of the spouses in AA were really adhering to the twelve steps just as their Al-Anon partners. Their marriages were showing real progress and were on the mend.

Not so in Norma and Kenny's case however. Step 11 of the twelve steps had been Norma's eye-opener. "God's will for *my* life," she had said.

Norma specifically had begun praying for God's will for her life and the courage to carry it out. She hadn't considered what was best for her in a very long time, if ever. It was a real awakening and felt so good, but it had not gone over well with Kenny. He controlled Norma's every move, and even though Norma had begun trying to make her own choices, Kenny had just become more and more abusive.

Libby pondered this and shared her plan to leave the hospital and never look back. She didn't know where she was going but knew she couldn't bring her to that house. She wanted her daughter to be safe.

As much as she hated it, she had told Norma she was even willing to go to a battered women's shelter until she could get on her feet. She had to turn the page on the chapter she was currently living and move on. That was clear.

"I know I am ready, Mom. I will be okay."

Libby told her that if she stayed with Jerry, being okay wouldn't even be a possibility. It felt good to her to even dare to hope for that possibility that she would one day be safe, away from Jerry, away from Kenny, really safe. Was that a sin? Reading Wayne Dyer's book *I Can See Clearly Now* (bibliotherapy assignment from Helen) had helped her to believe that her marriage to Jerry was simply a stepping-stone and wanting to move on was merely the next step.

Norma admitted to not being able to leave Kenny until she really let the eleventh step sink in. That she also deserved a safe and happy life.

"We were trying to be good Christians, Libby. We loved our neighbor, or spouse, as the case may be. We just forgot to love ourselves in the process. I finally heard that small, still voice, honey. I know it was Holy Spirit telling me it is time to move on to the next chapter of my life. I wanted a relationship with you, and I wanted to feel safe. That's when I found the courage to turn the page."

Her mother admitted to her that she "always felt uncomfortable when you and Daddy spent so much time together. The truth was there all the time somewhere deep within my subconscious."

Norma had been genuine in her tearful apology. Libby had told her she forgave her fully and wanted to focus on the good that was happening with them now. Her mother gladly agreed.

Libby remembered reading in her Bible that all evil would eventually be brought into the light. Helen had told her that as well. And her mom had confirmed it today. Today's visit had been full of light.

The pains were unbearable now. Libby braced herself against the steering wheel and sucked in her breath, letting it out slowly, trying to stay focused on the breathing techniques she had learned in Lamaze class. In between the contractions, she drifted in and out of sleep. "Please, God, please. We need a miracle."

Her thoughts drifted again to the afternoon tea with her mother and having a new daughter to share her life with. She shared in her mother's hope that this new life might indeed soften her grandmother's heart. She needed these happy thoughts to keep her focused on the good. They had reconnected and were going to make a new life for themselves.

During their visit, Norma had told Libby, "Your grandmother never asked about personal things about your father. Nothing about manners, behaviors, personality, drinking habits. And I never even tried to get to know Jerry precisely because of his drinking so heavily that day at the barbeque. I was so scared for you, Libby. I didn't want for you the pain I had suffered because of Kenny's drinking."

"Helen would have called that learned helplessness, Mama. It is a theory developed by Carol Hooker—that if you get knocked down enough times, you just don't have the strength to get back up anymore, not without help, that is. It makes a lot of sense," Libby offered.

"My fear of being disowned by your grandmother was every bit as strong as her fear of losing her status in the community," Norma had said sadly. She stated that she loved her mother and wished that they could someday have the kind of relationship that she and Libby were intent on building.

"Except for her poker friends and, of course, me and Maria, Mother just shut down after Daddy died. She didn't give a flip about the charity boards anymore. It think it took Daddy's death for her to realize what was really important in life."

Libby nodded. "And you and I had already become estranged." Libby had cried softly. "What a mess we made trying to be someone else's idea of who we were supposed to be."

Presently, she said, "But now we have another change, don't we, God, another chapter?" Libby sat there under her blanket with the bright-red, blue, and gold embroidery, remembering when her mother had given it to her.

An old Native American woman had sewn the blanket's finishing touches on it at a powwow that Norma attended in Cherokee, North Carolina. The woman had given Norma a blessing, telling her the blanket had its own purpose and she would know it soon enough.

Norma had told Libby she felt goose bumps when that beautiful, wrinkled old woman had handed her the blanket. She had been very quiet, yet very serious as she said it. The words had been an extraordinary omen of some kind. Norma had been sure of it. And now it was protecting Libby and her daughter from the freezing temperature outside.

Libby was shivering from the cold. She had told her mother everything, including the horrific shame she felt every time her father had violated her. Norma had been so angry and wept so deeply.

"What good is all of this honesty now?" Libby had cried out to God. "It has to work together for good. It has to." As she reached to adjust the car heater, she felt another contraction and the need to push. She couldn't help herself. It felt like her whole body was coming apart. "This baby is coming. God, we need that miracle." Then she passed out.

She awoke with another contraction and the need to push. "Breathe, just breathe." She breathed slowly and remembered her last words to Jerry before he had hit her and stumbled off to bed.

"We need to divorce, Jerry. You are not happy. I am not happy. You clearly don't want our daughter, and you don't want me. I don't know why you even stay here."

He had punched her in the stomach. *It had been a terrible path to freedom*, Libby thought. *But I consider it an open door, God, and I'm determined to walk through it if you will spare me and my child.* Libby continued to pray, "Dear God, I don't believe that all the good that is happening right now is for naught. Mama and me finally connecting and on the total honesty level I've always wanted. I trust you. We will be okay. All things will work together for good. They will."

Libby refused to give in to her anxiety, which was quickly turning to panic. She soothed herself, moment by moment, by placing her trust in God and moving out of the way so that the burden of what might happen next was not on her shoulders. She marveled at the calmness that settled upon her.

She turned on the radio to pass the time. She prayed constantly that someone would soon see her car lights and stop to help. She knew that it would have to be a miracle as it was the middle of the night and most people were at home, off these icy roads, or at least inside at a party.

It was getting hard to focus on anything at this point. She heard an announcement that caused her to bolt upright.

"Father Tom Yancey, a former parish priest, had just returned to this area and was struck down by a hit-and-run driver just a few hours ago…had emergency surgery and although he is in recovery, he remains in critical condition."

Libby couldn't believe it. That was the same priest that her mother had been such close friends with for years before she had married Libby's father. Libby knew he had been a guest at their dinner table for many years and had seemed like such a nice person. Father Tom had been her mother's best friend. It had come as a complete surprise to everyone in the parish community when he abruptly left town the day after her mama and daddy got married.

Church officials said he was transferring to another parish in another state. Oddly, nobody knew for certain where he had gone. Libby did ask her mother once, "What happed to the other priest we had before I was born?" Norma had gotten very quiet and said, "We didn't own him here, Libby. He had to go where he was being called."

CHAPTER 2

L ibby had no idea how long she'd been asleep. The engine was still running. She had awakened to a man pounding on her window asking if she was okay.

She sat up and shut off the engine. With his help, she climbed out of the car, but just as she did, another hard contraction hit. She doubled over in pain.

"Help me, please," Libby had whispered, barely audible at this point.

The man who had rescued her was a doctor, and he said he had seen her emergency lights.

"That's the only reason I was able to see you in the ditch, but you are going to be okay."

"Thank you, Holy Spirit," Libby whispered.

The doctor explained that he was a surgeon at Transylvania Hospital in Brevard. He had just finished a very difficult operation on a hit-and-run victim. He shook his head. "The driver was long gone by the time the police arrived at the scene. The man is lucky to be alive. And it turns out, young lady, so are you."

Libby explained to him that she was in labor and had been driving herself to the hospital when her car spun on the ice and rolled into the ditch.

"As I said before, you're damned lucky. I see you are wearing a wedding ring. Where is your husband? Why isn't he with you at a time like this?"

Libby didn't want the doctor to know anything about her problems with Jerry, so she told him her husband was out of town. When asked if there was anyone he could call to meet them at the hospital, Libby hesitated, then said, "Call my mother, Norma Vault," and gave him the number.

The man had introduced himself as Dr. George Leonard. He then proceeded to dial the number Libby had provided for him.

The answering machine came on, and a voice said, "You have reached Kenny and Norma Vault."

Libby grabbed the phone and quickly hung up. "My father, I don't want him to know," she explained.

Dr. Leonard was confused and surprised. "I know that name," he said as he scratched his head. "I bought a time share from him a few years ago when I lived in Orlando. It was not a good experience." He did not like this man, Kenny Vault. Then he became suspicious of Libby's circumstances. "You weren't out here trying to kill yourself, were you? I might want to with a father like yours. My interactions with him were not pleasant."

Libby had another contraction. "I promise you, no," she screamed. "But you are right. My father is not a kind man. In fact, he is an evil man and it would just make things worse if he knew. Please don't call him back," she pleaded with tears streaming down her face.

Dr. Leonard told her he intended to help her and her baby. That was his only concern. "Please get in the back seat of your car now."

She did as she was told, trusting, grateful for any help.

Kindly, the doctor explained what he was doing. "You have dilated ten centimeters, young lady. Your baby is coming." He could see the bruising on Libby's abdomen and asked what happened.

"This is why I was driving myself to the hospital," Libby explained. "I am sorry I lied to you. My name is Libby. I didn't know if I could trust you. This is not the first time. I am leaving my husband. As you can see, he is an abusive man. I am so sorry for lying to you. It isn't something I do lightly. I hope you will try to understand."

"I don't make judgments, Libby. Whatever is going on with you and your husband is none of my business, but the abuse cannot continue. Do you understand? I'll report it myself if necessary." The young doctor was working gently, yet firmly, trying to turn the baby around. "Your baby is breach," he said softly. "I'm going to give you something to help with the pain." He gave Libby a shot and continued with the delivery.

Leonard was a surgeon, but he hadn't delivered a baby in years. Not since the death of his wife. There was a car accident. She had been expecting their first child. He was driving. Neither had survived.

He had suffered terribly with depression and had wondered if he would ever be able to go on living without his wife and their unborn child. When he was finally able to return to work, he had made the decision to sell his private practice in Orlando and had been blessed with an appointment at Transylvania Hospital in Brevard, North Carolina. It was a small but modern hospital with very up-to-date equipment and a staff of fine doctors and nurses. He was grateful for the second chance.

Libby was stirring. He sedated her again and started back to work. He begged God to give him the opportunity to save this baby, if that were even possible. Tears stung his eyes as he thought of his own baby.

He had been driving home from the movies that horrible night. Ironically, it was snowing then too. He received a concussion from the accident. The car had spun out of control, and he had hit a tree. It had broken his heart that he hadn't been able to help the EMTs.

They had told him as soon as he was alert that Cindy didn't make it and the baby was too premature. Both had died before the ambulance could reach the hospital. And George had lost everything that meant anything to him. He felt responsible, and the guilt was still heavy on his heart.

It took several hours, but this stranger's baby finally turned. Dr. Leonard wiped away tears of gratitude as he handed the baby girl to her mother. He placed her gently upon Libby's chest under the blanket she had refused to let go of, a very intricately woven Native American design.

"Thank God I put those chains on this morning," he said to himself.

Carefully, George Leonard drove Libby and her daughter to the hospital. He had already called the ER and attendants were waiting to take over. His job was done, and he was very tired.

Libby woke up when they placed her on the stretcher, and she squeezed Dr. Leonard's hand. "Please stay with me," she whispered. He promised he would. He explained to the paramedics that it had been a difficult delivery and the baby had been breach. He said he had been a passerby and "saw the woman's emergency lights on." He wanted to make sure she way okay.

Libby was grateful that he had not mentioned anything about the bruises on her abdomen. They would ask about them soon enough.

Once Libby had been taken upstairs and he knew she was in good hands, he felt his whole body relax. Tired as he was from the surgery of the hit-and-run victim and now delivering this baby girl, he was determined to grant her wish. He had felt so grateful to have been of help to her and her baby. She seemed to sense it.

He waited in the lobby until his colleague came out and said, "They're going to be just fine. You can see them now. And could you please assist the mom in filling out the proper paperwork? She shook her head and refused to look at them when I handed them to her."

Libby smiled as Dr. Leonard walked into the room. "You saved our lives, Doctor."

He smiled back. "Maybe I did that," he said happily. "By the way, please call me George."

About that time, the doctor's cell phone rang. It was Kenny Vault.

"You called my phone a few hours ago in the middle of the night for God's sake! What can I do for you?"

George looked at Libby, then turned back to the caller. "I dialed you in error, Mr. Vault. So sorry to have disturbed you." When he hung up, he spoke gently to Libby. "You don't need any more stress tonight. We have an unpleasant history, your father and me. It involves a time-share he badgered me into buying shortly after my wife and baby died. The media is out there. He will know soon enough that I delivered your baby." George sat down next to Libby. "Do you want to tell me now why you don't want him to know you were in labor? This will probably be in the papers tomorrow and likely on the news tonight. It's not every day the first New Year's baby is born in a ditch, you know."

"Yes, you are right, but please give me some time. I'm very tired, and I'm sure you are anxious to get home. Your wife must be worried sick."

George hadn't told many people about Cindy and didn't know why he wanted to tell Libby, but he did. He wanted to tell her everything.

"I'll make you a deal. I'll tell you why I have no one to go home to and you can tell me why you have a husband and father you want to hide from. But you do need some rest. I'll come back tomorrow after I make my rounds. Until then my lips are sealed."

Libby smiled, then grabbed his hand. "I do want my mom to know. I just gave you the home number by mistake. When my father answered, I freaked! My husband stole my cell phone, so I couldn't call her. I will call her soon, I promise. Does the hospital staff know who I am?"

George assured her they did not. He had just told them there was a "car in a ditch, a woman in labor, a baby delivered with the complication of a breech position and paperwork would have to wait." To Libby, he said, "I must tell you though. They are pressing me to help you complete the admission forms." He told Libby that he remembered seeing a purse in the car. "Do you want me to get it for you? I could bring it tomorrow morning."

Libby shook her head. "You are so kind and generous. That would be great. Thank you. I promise you, if you will just give me tonight to rest, I will tell you everything tomorrow morning."

"Me too," he said, feeling stirring within himself that he had not felt for years. "George Leonard," he murmured to himself as he walked out of the room. "You have just delivered a healthy baby girl, and you are strongly attracted to her very mysterious mother." Then he thought as he walked out of the hospital, *The priest is going to be okay as well. It has been a good night.*

On his way back to Libby's car, he replayed finding her in the ditch. Over and over, his mind relived every detail. She had been so grateful. Little did she know that his successful delivery of her child was such a huge blessing to him. Interesting and a little mysterious was the fact that her father had once lived in Orlando, Florida, at the same time Dr. Leonard had.

Bringing that baby into this world brought me back to life, he thought and said a silent thank you to God. *And her mom is gorgeous, yet something isn't right in her world. That's for sure.*

George saw a convertible parked at the end of the road but didn't see anyone in the car.

Someone else stranded, he thought, thankful that they had probably had someone pick them up.

He walked over to Libby's car and at once felt something hard in his back. It felt like a gun.

"Don't turn around," the voice was clear. "Do you know the owner of this car?"

George lied. "I saw it in the ditch and thought I'd offer my help." Jerry had come to get Libby's purse but wasn't about to tell this man anything.

What the hell is this guy doing here at Libby's car? Jerry thought. *Libby has some answering to do.* He hit the doctor over the head with his gun. He hadn't realized how hard he had hit him until the man went down, hard, into the ditch. Then he took Libby's purse from the car and headed to Transylvania Hospital leaving the other man to die.

Jerry had awakened a couple hours after Libby had left and had flown into a jealous rage when he saw that she was gone.

"She had better not be screwing around on me." Then he smiled. "The woman is nine months pregnant, you fool. Who would want her?"

It hadn't taken him long to remember how hard he had hit her in the stomach, so he went looking for her. He really didn't mean to hit her so hard, but she had really pissed him off.

"Why did she keep doing that?"

He was surprised that Libby had told him she wanted a divorce. Another abandonment! Not that he really wanted to be married to her. He loved Kenny. But he tried to be a decent man, a decent husband. He had even remembered some of the Bible verses his foster grandmother had taught him, and in the beginning he had enjoyed talking to Libby about her faith in God. He never really felt comfortable sharing his faith with Kenny.

But the thought of her making the decision to leave rather than him leaving her, "How dare she? Who does she think she is?" He realized he was shaking. He sure didn't want her dead, just out of his life.

If she is dead, the murder would be pinned on me for sure, he thought. *But she's not dead. That man knows something. I wouldn't be surprised if he knew Libby.*

He was worried as he hadn't yet heard whether his hit-and-run victim was found dead or alive. And now he had injured another man.

Where was the God his foster grandmother used to tell him about? The God that lets the rain fall on the just and the unjust, the sunshine on the good and the wicked? He had only known storms. Jerry wiped away a tear as he thought of his love for Kenny. He just wanted Kenny to come out of the closet, to love him openly. He had begged him to leave Norma and marry him. What was so wrong with that? Tired of living a lie. Jerry wanted the whole world to know that he and Kenny were lovers. Jerry even prayed about it at least weekly!

He wanted Kenny to go to church with him, but Kenny was afraid someone might recognize him. Jerry attended a Unitarian church. He didn't like the fact that they rarely talked about God's grace or Jesus, but at least he could be openly gay there.

Jerry never forgot his foster grandmother's words though, that God would always love him, no matter what, and had often studied Christian literature. He liked the philosophical things he was learning at the Unitarian church though, and so wished that Kenny would go with him! He knew people suspected, but he had promised Jerry he wouldn't tell anyone, and he had kept that promise.

No wonder I'm so angry all the time, Jerry thought. *It's not like I don't try to live right! God knows I try. If we'd just talk about some of the stuff that makes us hurt so bad, instead of trying to impress each other with our latest sexual slips, we might get somewhere.*

Jerry really liked his AA group and was learning a lot there about himself and about others. The particular group he attended really worked the twelve steps. He liked that. He hated the Sexaholics Anonymous meetings. As far as Jerry could see, it was just a place to learn new ways of having sex, new places that hadn't yet been explored. But that is where he met Kenny, and he went for Kenny. Jerry would do anything for Kenny. He would sell his business and run away with him.

When he saw Libby's car in the ditch, he had hoped that she and the baby were dead inside. Not because he was uncaring. She was a good person and actually more of a true friend than Kenny because she listened to him and genuinely cared when he was hurting or sick. She was smart too and had a deep faith in God, which had surprised Jerry since Kenny obviously attended church for show.

"Never know when I might pick up a client," he would say to Jerry. "Church is a good place to meet people," but he would only attend church with his precious wife and daughter, not with Jerry.

It wasn't that Jerry hated Libby. He had actually grown fond of her as a person because she understood him. He just resented Kenny's obsession with her. She was all he ever talked about.

As time went on, it was just too much for Jerry listening to Libby telling him how much she loved him and expecting him to actually love her. He felt pressured because she was so damn accommodating. He did grow quite close to her and was actually sorry he took his anger out on her; but he could never love anyone, male or female, more than he loved Kenny. And that was something he could never tell Libby!

The car was empty, and it was clear Libby was nowhere to be found.

Someone must have stopped to help and taken her to the hospital, he thought.

He called Norma to see if Libby had called her. Norma kept up the pretense that she hadn't seen her daughter since she and Jerry married. He pretended to believe her and hung up abruptly. He checked her purse to see if she had taken any money. A few twenties. He took them and stuffed them in his pocket, thinking, *If she plans to leave me, she will just have to leave my money as well.*

Meanwhile, Norma put down the phone, took a deep breath and let it out slowly. She knew Jerry was abusive to Libby. She knew Jerry was an alcoholic and was unfaithful sexually.

"Why in the world is he trying to find her in the middle of the night?" Norma wondered. Her intuition shouted within, *She is in trouble, and you have to find her.*

Grabbing her purse and car keys, Norma headed to the hospital. When she got there, she saw Jerry's car. She grimaced but was more worried about Libby than anything Jerry might do or say to her.

Jerry had gotten to the hospital a few minutes before Norma. He had told the staff his wife was missing, and he had found her car in a ditch.

"Could she possibly have been admitted?"

The nurse smiled. "Not only was she admitted, you have a healthy baby girl. Blond hair and blue eyes. She takes after her mother. You're not going to believe this, but she was born in a ditch. Thank God one of our doctors saw your wife's car on his way home. She could have frozen to death or died giving birth, but mother and daughter are fine. I'm sorry I am rambling on so, but it isn't every day we get to be a part of something like this. Would you like to see them now?"

Jerry appeared grief-stricken that his wife and daughter might have died. "They're going to be okay, right?" he asked.

The nurse nodded as he followed her down the hall to Libby's room.

"That's wonderful news," he whispered bitterly. Part of him was really glad they weren't dead, but part of him wished they were. "I hate my life," he said to himself as he followed the nurse. "I hate my life."

When they walked into the room, Libby stifled a scream. It did not go unnoticed by the nurse. Jan Turner had been a nurse for twenty-five years. She knew fear when she saw it.

"Are you okay, sweetie?" she asked carefully. "You look like you've seen a ghost."

Libby pulled her hand away from her mouth as Jerry sat down on the bed. "Just surprised is all," she said slowly as she turned to Jerry. "How did you know I was here?"

Jerry told her about waking up and finding her gone and how worried he was. He told her about finding her car and how he had panicked when he didn't see her in it. "Yeah, yeah. I heard that doctor came just in the nick of time."

Libby kept quiet. She didn't want Jerry to find out the identity of her rescuer or any of the details surrounding the baby's birth.

Norma walked in shortly after Jerry walked out. Libby told her to close the door, then told her the same story. Norma said she knew something was wrong when he had called her looking for Libby, pretending to be worried.

"I thought I'd find you in the morgue," Norma cried. "Your father is out, honey. He doesn't know anything yet. Thank God you are okay. How is that precious little bundle?"

Libby handed her daughter to her mother. She then told her about the breech birth and the kindness of Dr. Leonard. She told her she was so thankful her daughter had been born "after I left that house of pain rather than birth her inside it."

Norma put her head in her hands and sobbed. "I am so sorry I raised you in a house of pain, Libby. Because he never touched you, never physically abused you, or at least I thought he hadn't, I put up with his abuse of me. Mother convinced me it was best for you to grow up with two parents no matter how horrible the home life was."

Tears ran down Libby's cheeks as well. "Mama, Daddy abused me from the time I was nine years old." She knew she had already admonished her mother earlier at her house, but she just couldn't let it go, not yet. It would take time, she realized, for her feelings to catch up to her decision to forgive her mother. Libby's therapist called it cognitive dissonance.

"How could you have not known? How? It is the reason I stayed with Jerry. He didn't hit me in the beginning. He yelled at me plenty, but only when he was drunk. I was used to it with you and Daddy. I hated it but figured I could handle it because you had. I felt trapped. I couldn't come home. I couldn't, Mama. I couldn't bear Daddy's hands on me another moment. Why couldn't you see it?"

Norma was patient. She knew it would take Libby a while to trust her, to know in her heart that she was indeed sorry. The two of them held each other for a long time and wept softly. Again, Libby was glad for her mother's arms and hated bringing up what she truly wanted to forgive.

When Libby finally pulled away, Norma said, "We can't change the past, honey, but I want you to know that I will spend the rest of my life standing beside you, listening to you, helping you to be all that you can be. I intend to be happy as well. We will both heal, Libby. Please tell me that is still possible at this point. Please tell me it isn't too late for you, for us."

Libby had nodded. "Yes, we will both heal. And now we have little Cody to join our circle of love. Good from evil, Mama. She is literally good from evil. God was with us the whole time. We just didn't know it because we were so focused on trying to make our marriages work. We both have been codependent in the decisions we have made with our husbands and you with Grandmother. We have both been who they wanted us to be, without even considering who we wanted to be. It has been horrible, unbearable at times. But the horror became so bad, it became the catalyst I needed to leave. I remember you telling me that God promises us that all things work together for good for those who love God and are called out according to His purposes! Cody is the good that came from all that bad. And I'm ready to be called out to His next purpose for me." She laughed as she said it but was dead seriousness.

"Yes, Libby. She definitely is good from evil." Norma smiled. "I am glad that both of us have already begun the healing process. I am glad that we are both seeing Helen. I know I have learned a lot about myself. I am sure you have as well. My little girl has a little girl of her own. And you are so smart, Libby. You always have been. Knowledge is good. Now we pray for wisdom. Knowledge without wisdom is nothing."

Libby surprised herself when she asked the question she had been wanting to ask for so long. "Mama, you have spent your entire life trying to please Grandmother. I know you married Daddy because of Grandmother's insistence. I heard you two arguing about Daddy and Father Tom a couple of times and never understood why she hated Father Tom so much and why she loved Daddy so much. Why didn't you just leave him long ago and take me with you? Why didn't you?"

Norma swallowed hard. "I should never have married your father, Libby. It isn't that mother loves Kenny. It's his family's money and status that she loves. His family in Florida are from very old money as far back as he can remember. They own so much stock in a time-share there. He thinks he owns it himself. He is very controlling, Libby, as you know. And I have lived with that kind of behavior for as long as I can remember. I didn't have the guts to stand up to him or to Mother. My life revolved around their wishes. Well, maybe once, I stood up to Grandmother when we were arguing about Father Tom," she said wistfully, "albeit ever so briefly. I will answer your question about him, but not now. I promise it will be soon, okay?

When we are at our new home, sipping a hot cup of chamomile tea, we will make it a tradition. Teatime weekly, if at all possible, will be our time to come together and get to know each other all over again."

Libby smiled. She wanted all the time she could get with her mother. "Weekly appointments with my mom. How cool is that?"

"By the way, did you know Father Tom is back in town? He is the hit-and-run victim they brought in a few hours before I got here." Her mother's voice trailed off as she remembered their last embrace. How she ran her fingers through his thick, curly blond hair before she left.

It was clear to Libby that her mother was glad to know that Father Tom was back in town and going to be okay. She knew her mother would keep her word. She also knew that just saying what she had said to Libby was quite painful. She let it go knowing that it was her mother's choice, but thinking it would be good to talk about it whatever it was, as it obviously still upset her to even think about it.

Norma touched Cody's hair. "She looks just like you, Libby, with the thick blond hair and gorgeous blue eyes. She seems to take after my side of the family. I remember my nana had blonde hair and deep blue eyes as well. She is so precious, Libby. So very precious. As I was saying, my codependency landed me in a marriage that was not only unhappy but, as it turns out, dangerous to both of us. I also think there is a part of us all that falls into the codependency trap on occasion. Helen and I discussed this as well. It makes sense. All the conflicting parts of us, trying to get their needs met simultaneously.

"I grew to depend on your grandmother to make all my decisions for me. I hated it, but after a while I began to believe that I really couldn't make good decisions for myself. It took its toll on me. To not be able to even get the haircut I wanted, right up to the week before I married your father. I can't believe that I didn't just go ahead and do what I wanted to do, for goodness sake. I had just numbed out, and whatever Mother said, I did. It was awful. I didn't know if I was happy or not. If Mother was pleased with me, I felt happy. If she wasn't, I felt sad and lost. My feelings fluctuated with Grandmother's moods."

Libby was thinking about the night before her own wedding, her own sense of helplessness. She realized she and her mother had something in common there, although Libby's rebellious side won out. She consciously chose to marry Jerry out of rebellion against her mother, her father, and her grandmother. And Norma had felt forced to marry Kenny.

"I was the rebellious one." Libby smiled. "You were right about Jerry, but I couldn't listen. I believed I'd be happy with him because he was going to take me away from the shame I had lived with for so long. Little did I know that those feelings of shame would follow me, and I would be right back in the same world of alcohol and abuse and sexual infidelity that you were enduring. And God, the STDs were humiliating. You believed you might be happy with Daddy because you wouldn't have to put up with Grandmother's controlling nature anymore. I believed I would be happy with Jerry because we both had abusive childhoods. Our own little 'support group.'" She laughed. "It seemed like a good idea then." Then she got serious. "We both married for the wrong reasons, Mama, but we did choose to love. We did our best. No regrets. We will focus on the future and deposit some heaping good memories into our own emotional bank accounts."

Norma laughed remembering how Helen had used those same words when she was teaching Norma some tools from the Gottman Marriage Institute. Making emotional deposits and carefully observing withdrawals was a very insightful tool and something that Libby practiced once per week. Norma had already begun using the tool in her interactions with Grandmother. Both Libby and Norma had been pleased with the results.

"Yes, we did do our best. You are right, Libby. We have nothing to be ashamed of. No guilt. No regrets. And for our own emotional health, we must always remember that neither of us asked to be abused. There is no excuse for staying a victim of any kind of violence. Pinky promise? From this day forward, Libby, we need to remember that we are survivors, not victims, okay?"

Libby extended her pinky finger as her mother wrapped it into her own pinky. This was a tradition since Libby was a little girl. One of the very good memories Libby chose to remember.

"We chose to stand by our man. Remember that Tammy Wynette song?" Norma smiled. "We did that as long as we could and still keep our sanity. We will work on forgiveness and wish them well. We have just reached a point where we need to wish them well from a distance."

Libby laughed. "Yes, I remember singing along with you every time you played Tammy Wynette's CD. We were trying to do the Christian thing, and that's not a bad thing. Like you said, we just forgot to love ourselves in the process. Our intentions were admirable. God knew our hearts. We were trying to love, forgive, and focus on the good. Isn't that the way we experience God? Remember we discussed that book by Marianne Williamson? I think it's true. We just forgot to include ourselves in the process. God wanted us to. We were just so tired, Mama, just so tired trying to please Daddy and Jerry and Grandmother! Don't know about you, but all that effort pulled me further and further away from God!"

"Me too, Libby. That's because we didn't know how to love ourselves the way God so yearned for us to." Norma continued,

"We are not sick women. We are pretty strong women. We have just been fighting an internal and external war that could not have possibly ended well, because there shouldn't have to be sides. In a healthy marriage, the two truly become one relationship, each taking into consideration how their decisions will affect the other, always. When you are forced to think about sides, love loses its power. Well, no more. It is time to turn the page and become vulnerable, which means telling the truth to Grandmother."

Libby laughed because her mother made it sound like she was going to face the devil herself.

Norma had already begun praying that God would soften her mother's heart where Libby was concerned, but now she dared to hope that the three of them could become close, even though she would follow through with divorcing Kenny. She also prayed that Cody would be accepted.

"It doesn't hurt that she looks like my nana." She smiled as Cody squeezed her pinky finger. "And she already knows the pinky promise."

Libby nodded. "I'm praying too, Mama. It will all work out. I just know it will. Cody is our little miracle. The sweetest, most beautiful baby girl waiting for us. For all of us. I think even Grandmother's heart will melt when she meets this little one."

Norma had been rocking her granddaughter and was now smiling down at her, so excited to be a nana. So grateful that she was even there with Libby at all. So hopeful that the future would, indeed, be much brighter for all of them.

"By the way, I have to ask, were you thinking of the term codependence in any way when you named this child?"

Libby grinned. "Yes, I was, but in a good way. Every time I say her name, Mama, I will remember that codependency is not a negative label the way some think. Nor is it something to be ashamed of. It is just part of us using inappropriate ways to try and meet legitimate needs. I agree with Helen that most, if not all, of us struggle with tendencies towards codependent behavior throughout our life."

Norma nodded.

Libby continued, "I will tell her one day that is where her name came from when the time is right. Holy Spirit will tell me when the time is right. When the time comes, when she is old enough, if and only if I feel led by God, she will know the circumstances of her conception. I hate for that day to come, but I vow to be truthful to Cody, and to you, and to Grandmother from this day forward, no matter how hard it is on me. I won't always succeed. As you said, we are imperfect beings and we will argue and say hurtful things to each other. But we will have our teas to talk about what hurt. I really like the idea, Mama. But if I do ever have to tell Cody the full circumstances of her conception, she will know that she is good from evil, joy from sadness, light from darkness, a beacon of hope. I want her to reject shame and the havoc it can wreak in one's life. I'm going to name her Cody Marie Williamson. The Williamson comes from the road she was born on, Williamson Creek. And, of course, Marie comes from a long line of family nanas. I will not give her Jerry's last name, and I don't want her to have my maiden name. I hope you can understand."

"Of course, I understand." Norma nodded. "Is that legal? Never mind. I don't care. And, yes, we will make sure Cody wears her name proudly."

"We will certainly be better role models for her now that we are seeing Helen. I am so glad that you are seeing her too, Mama. I hope that one day we can see her together."

"Of course, dear. I owe that woman a lot more that her counseling fee. And I am willing to do whatever it takes to bring about healing within this family." She laughed then and said with a grin, "But I can't do it alone. I know that now. And, of course, we can't lose ourselves in the process."

Libby laughed too. "We are learning, Mama. We are learning."

"And we will keep on learning," Norma replied.

Norma gently laid Cody in her mother's arms and said, "A beautiful name for a beautiful girl. I am in love with her already. Did you see the way she squeezed my finger? And don't tell me it's an instinctive reflex. This child knows the pinky promise, and she knows I am going to spoil her rotten."

Libby smiled. She was so grateful for the scene before her. Her mama lovingly kissing her daughter. She felt bittersweet tears in her eyes.

"Mama, I doubt very seriously that Jerry will ever be back or even bother to find out her name. I wonder though, since you mentioned it, if it is legal to give her a different last name? Her name is an important beginning for her and for me. I'll take my chances regarding the legality of it all."

Norma shook her head. "I don't know, sweetie. I really don't. I doubt she is Jerry's child as she is so fair skinned. Of course, she doesn't look Puerto Rican either. She looks like you and she looks like my nana. I can see that clearly. And for now, let's let that be enough!"

Libby smiled. Thank God for another miracle. She did find it odd though that Cody didn't have even one physical characteristic of her father. He had brown hair and an olive complexion and was indeed attractive. His skin was even darker that Jerry's though, which Libby found ironic. But Grandmother had approved of him because he wasn't a Negro. He was Puerto Rican and from a very affluent Puerto Rican family.

Libby smiled, thankful that Cody had no similarities to Kenny. Then she became quite serious.

"Can you look through Daddy's law books, discreetly, of course. I don't think her name will be a problem, unless Jerry demands a paternity test."

"Do you think he will?" Norma asked.

Libby felt sure he wouldn't. "He has no interest in Cody."

"Okay then." Norma breathed a sigh of relief. "I'll be back tomorrow, my dear daughter." She gathered her belongings, kissed the top of Libby's head, held Cody's finger one more time and said, "I will be forever grateful for our reconnection at Quotations. We'll have to take Cody there sometime."

Chapter 3

Jerry sped down Asheville Highway. He was furious. Libby had seemed awfully quiet when he mentioned the doctor who had helped her. "What if she has been screwing him all along?" His jaw clenched in anger. He was surprised that he cared so much. He really did like her, but he couldn't very well tell her he was in love with her father!

He parked the Mercedes in the driveway and pondered what to do about Libby's car. He didn't want to get it fixed but didn't want it sitting in his driveway either. Just as he was about to turn the ignition off, he heard an announcement on the radio all about Dr. George Leonard saving Libby and her baby from certain death had he not found them when he did.

"Had the good doctor not been called in to perform emergency surgery on a hit-and-run victim, he would not have been in the right place at the right time, and mother and daughter would surely be dead."

The news announcer went on to report how the doctor had gone back to the car to retrieve Libby's purse, as it was on his way home. When he got to the car, he had been hit with a blunt object. The driver of a tow truck had found him in the ditch right beside the car he was sent to retrieve from the ditch on Williamson Creek Road.

If it hadn't been daylight, Cooper, from Brevard Towing Services, would have never seen him.

"Great, now they know about that too. What else do they know?" Jerry began to sweat. "Has Libby told them anything? Not likely. She knows how to keep quiet," he told himself as he brushed snow of his windshield. "I guess I should be grateful for that."

He had wanted to leave Libby's car in the ditch, but the hospital nurse knew that he was aware of the accident. So he had reluctantly called a tow truck and had the car taken to Brevard Tire.

"Do they know I'm the one that hit the doctor? Do they know that I hit that priest? Do they know about me hitting Libby? Are they going to come after me now?" He kept asking himself the same questions over and over again. Almost in a panic. Jerry thought about calling Kenny. Angrily, he kicked the front door open. "One more problem to deal with," he said to himself.

He vaguely recalled having one too many and hitting the pedestrian. He knew he had hurt him pretty badly but had been afraid to stay with him. His blood alcohol level was over the top. He knew he would be arrested, and they would put two and two together.

Terrified, Jerry acknowledged to himself and to God that his drinking was out of control. Was it too late for him? Kenny was spending less and less time with him.

It was all so perfect, Jerry thought. *Why did he have to marry Norma? Why couldn't he have been happy with me?*

He sat down and sobbed. He and Kenny had been lovers for years ever since they met in Orlando, outside the Sexaholics Anonymous meeting. Kenny was attending there. He was just a kid when they met. They were happy together, before they were fired and had to move to North Carolina. Kenny's father said he could come back to the law firm, and Kenny had helped Jerry get set up in his own business. Things were going well.

But then it all changed. Kenny met and married Norma. Then he had to make things worse by inviting Jerry to that stupid barbeque party! He had seen Libby with Jerry and had come up with the perfect plan, or so he had thought. But it was the beginning of the end for Jerry. Kenny had actually been excited with his plan. Jerry had thought it was sick.

"She's great in bed, Jerry. I've taught her lots of stuff. She's still my little girl, and I don't want to give her to just anybody," he had said. "If you marry her, I can spend a lot more time at your house and no one will question it because Libby's my daughter."

And so he had succumbed to Kenny's wishes and had married Libby. That way Jerry could "have Libby to play with when I'm not around. And who knows if I still want some of the action?" Kenny had slapped Jerry's back, thinking Jerry wouldn't mind.

But Jerry did mind. He didn't like the idea of Kenny "playing" with his wife. He did make it clear the night of his wedding that if Kenny was giving her to him, she was his and he didn't want to share her.

"If she's my wife, she's my wife," Jerry had stood up to Kenny angrily. Something he didn't often do. He didn't like the fact that Kenny had sexually abused his daughter. It reminded him of his own childhood abuse, so he told Kenny, "You don't touch her."

Kenny had been surprised but had nodded in agreement, and they shook hands on it. He had tried to get Jerry to change his mind a time or two, but Jerry was adamant. He had decided if Kenny was going to have a wife and keep playing house, so would he. He hated that Kenny was still so attached to Libby, but he would not "share" her.

As he wept, Jerry's mind went back to evenings with Libby in front of the fireplace. He would lay his head in her lap, stretch out on the sofa, while she rubbed his head and neck and read. Or they would talk for hours. He really enjoyed being with Libby, just not sexually. She had been a good listener, a good friend, someone with whom he could talk openly. At least about his childhood. And looking back, he felt like Libby really cared about him too. He knew she could identify with what he told her about his childhood. It was hard to talk about it, but she really cared about what he had to say. He wished it could be enough, but it wasn't and never would be.

"Why does the world have to be this way?" He continued to weep. "Why does Kenny need to present this happy heterosexual family? What is wrong with a happy homosexual family? Doesn't he realize how much he's hurting me?"

Libby had been pregnant when they married, and the sight of her growing belly disgusted Jerry, just as Norma's pregnancy had been a real turn off to Kenny. Jerry couldn't understand why any man would be attracted to that. But if she gave him a son, that would be great. It was something he thought of every day. A son would turn his life around. Someone he could love openly without pretense!

He was really excited about the possibility. He had dreams of being a better father to his son. Better than his old man had been to him. "Who knows?" he had mused. "Maybe I'll enjoy being a father." The thought was bittersweet though, because what he wanted more than anything else in the world was to be with Kenny, have their own home, and adopt their own children, or even get a surrogate.

Jerry had offered that idea to Kenny years ago. He had offered to be the sperm donor. Kenny had said he didn't want children and didn't want the marriage scene. Jerry remembered it like it was yesterday. "That's just not me, Jerry." So when Libby got pregnant, Jerry actually felt some excitement.

"Kenny had his chance to be a father, and he was lousy at it. I'll be different," he told himself. "My boy will get the best life has to offer, and Libby will be a good mother."

When the doctor broke the news to him and Libby that it was a girl, Jerry hadn't said one word. He just turned and walked out of the doctor's office. Libby followed in disbelief.

One more blow, Jerry had thought. *Can't I ever get a break?*

That was when he had hit her with the baseball bat as soon as they got home. It was just a hollow play bat. A toy for his son. What a letdown to find out there would be no son. And today, when she had suggested divorce, he had punched her in the stomach, without even thinking twice. Jerry knew it was a horrible thing to do, but he really couldn't help himself. He had been drunk after all. And Libby had provoked him as usual.

"Not my fault," he murmured to himself. Then felt sick as he remembered his own father saying the same words to him.

Jerry was aware that his head was spinning from too much alcohol, so he went to bed. That had become his pattern. When he woke up, he turned on the television. The story of the man Jerry had hit was all over the news. The man, it turned out, was the very same priest that Libby had told him about. The one that had been "such a good friend to my mother until she married Daddy."

He remembered Libby tearing up telling him that her mama had cried for weeks when she found out the priest had left their local parish and had moved to another state.

Why the hell is he back now? Jerry wondered.

He finally called Kenny and asked him to come over. "And bring some beer," he had snapped. "What I am about to tell you is not going to be good. In fact, it is life-changing, Kenny, life-changing."

Kenny was tired and really didn't want to go to Jerry's house. He cared for Jerry though, and Jerry was obviously distraught. So he decided to go and hear his friend out.

He and Jerry had been together longer than any other man Kenny had been with. They had worked together at the largest time-share company in the world before they both got fired. When they decided to move from Florida to North Carolina, things just fell into place for them. And he wasn't just his lover. He was his son-in-law too. So Kenny went to his friend.

On the drive over to Jerry's house, Kenny thought back to his job at Window to Your Dreams. Along with all the others in sales, they had swindled a lot of old geezers who were itching to spend their retirement money. Kenny was immune to the suffering of others, but not Jerry. Most of the people were elderly.

"Not my problem," Kenny had told Jerry when he had a weak moment and had asked how Kenny had felt about "taking all that retirement money for nothing other than an opportunity to search inventory that wouldn't be available when they really wanted it."

Jerry had genuinely felt sorry for all these elderly people. He thought it was wrong to persuade people to give up a good-sized chunk of their retirement money for a permit to search vacation places on the Internet for great prices with, of course, the enormous buy-in.

The company had taken millions from the elderly for years. And though it did bother Jerry at first, he had succumbed to the highs he got every time he made a sale. Kenny had been glad they could work together and celebrate their victories together. They were good friends.

Their sales team had the highest sales across the nation. They had helped make Window to Your Dreams rich beyond measure. Of course, they were selling more weeks than would ever be available should several owners choose the same resort at the same time, even if it was their home resort.

So it's a rip-off, Kenny was thinking. *But a damn good one.* He laughed to himself as he took the exit to Jerry's.

The original investment costs for the time-shares were exorbitant, not to mention the ongoing maintenance fees. It put good money into his and Jerry's pockets though, and that's what counts.

While waiting on Kenny to get there, Jerry began wishing he had Rafael's gun. Kenny said he's hidden it and hadn't mentioned it for a while. Jerry made up his mind. He wasn't going to be caught without a fight, should the cops find out what he had done. The guilt of it all was suffocating. First Libby, then the priest, then the doctor.

"God-awful mess," Jerry muttered under his breath. *I didn't mean to hurt anybody, God. I swear, I didn't.* Tears were forming in Jerry's eyes.

It was bad enough when he and Kenny had been let go from the time-share company. The CEO, Rick Browning, was suing them. Telling everyone that he didn't know they were so corrupt. He and Kenny were fired shortly after the company had been sued by Dr. George Leonard. It was all such a joke. And then the doctor shows up in Brevard, North Carolina.

"What are the chances of that happening again in this lifetime?"

The corporate headquarters pushed the salespeople to sell, sell, sell. The CEO, Rick Browning, knew they were being fraudulent in their selling practices. Hell, sometimes they even sold owners something below what they already owned or, worse, sold them something they already owned, just explained it from a different perspective without even blinking an eye.

The unsuspecting victims didn't know the difference, and Browning didn't care. The owners complained constantly though because they could rarely get a reservation at the place they really wanted to stay unless they paid their maintenance fees before they were due and booked a reservation thirteen months in advance. There were no guarantees.

Jerry was getting anxious. Kenny should be there by now. His thoughts continued to focus on their time in Florida. They had swindled a lot of people, but just being with Kenny every day and most nights made up for the fraudulent acts they were committing.

Rick Browning hadn't cared; neither had Kenny. After a while, Jerry also looked the other way. He wasn't proud of the fact he had performed dishonest acts for the company as a sales agent, their attorney, and, lastly, their accountant. He prided himself in the fact that he felt sorry for the owners.

"I can't help it if they fell for it," he would tell himself. "They're adults, and if they want to make stupid choices, that's their right."

Forcing himself back to the present, Jerry became aware that he was sweating profusely. "Hell, I could be up against several charges— battering, vehicular homicide, and assault with a deadly weapon." Jerry thought back over the last twenty-four hours. He became more and more agitated and wondered again what was keeping Kenny. He tried calling again, but his phone when straight to voice mail.

Jerry's mind went back to when he had first met the Dr. Leonard. He had truly felt sorry for him because his wife and unborn child had both died just a few weeks before. He had showed up with some friends who were trying to help him through the tragedy of losing his wife and baby. Jerry hated to take advantage of him because he knew how it felt to lose someone you love.

He had lost his mother; his father; and Raphael, his first love. He actually tried to talk Kenny out of that sale, but of course, Kenny would have none of his whining. He remembered how Kenny had badgered the poor doctor until he broke like all the rest.

The doc's wife and unborn baby had been in the car when they crashed. The doc had been driving and was still grieving acutely. He had told them that. He had also told them that he, at the suggestion of friends, had decided to check on time-share ownership. "It would be a good opportunity to get away for a while," Dr. Leonard's friend had told him. And that was why he had walked into their offices that morning.

Kenny was a shark. He was very self-confident, a trait that Jerry admired greatly. George Leonard was a cautious man, but he was so depressed about the accident he wasn't thinking straight. Jerry could see that. Even so, Kenny had pressed him hard.

The doctor had told him he didn't think he should invest so much money when he was in such an acute state of grief. But Kenny had feigned concern about his depression, had reiterated what the doc's friends had told him, and had even told him about the three-day money back guarantee if not satisfied. He rarely did that because most people didn't ask. Yes, it was in the paperwork, albeit in very fine print.

By the end of the day, the doctor had buckled and had bought a level of membership that was way beyond his monetary means. He walked out the owner of a beautiful time-share that could be used all over the US and even in Mexico and other countries, with the extra exchange rate, in addition to the annual maintenance fees, of course. Jerry grimaced as he remembered the doc walking out of their offices, his shoulders slumped.

Kenny had even gotten a bottle of champagne out of the office refrigerator and popped it open to celebrate. The doctor was so numb with sadness he didn't even drink with them. He just sat there. Jerry was wondering, even now, how Kenny could be so uncaring about it all.

"Unlike you, Kenny, I have a conscience," Jerry muttered out loud.

He remembered challenging Kenny about the whole thing after the doctor had gone. Kenny had yelled at him to "never question me or anything I do, ever again!" Jerry had never seen Kenny that mad before.

Three days later the doctor had come back in wanting to cancel his purchase. The paperwork said that he had three days to change his mind.

But Kenny had told the doctor, "Don't worry about the deadline, Dr. Leonard. Take all the time you need. We'll just let you think about it a little longer. You've been through a lot. There's no rush."

Kenny had talked the doctor into giving it a few more days, knowing fully that the time period to cancel would then be over. The doctor had walked out disgruntled but too depressed to argue with Kenny.

A week later the doc had come back. Due to his sister's insistence, Leonard, who admitted to being severely depressed, had tried to use his membership to get away for a while. That's when he had discovered that even though his membership was the VIP gold level, he couldn't get reservations at his home resort, which is where he really wanted to visit.

The doctor had been very angry. That's when Kenny had put his arm around the doc and said, "Buddy, you waited too long. You only had three days to change your mind, and you just took too long."

The doctor reminded Kenny of telling him to take a few more days, and Kenny had shrugged. "I don't remember that, sir, but I am sure you will enjoy your investment once you get over this bad break."

The doctor had punched Kenny right in the jaw. "I will never get over this," he had said, and he had walked out.

That following week Dr. Leonard had sue Window to Your Dreams for the exact amount of his investment and all legal fees.

That's when Jerry had gotten involved. Jerry was a good accountant, one of the best in the state. Having a law degree didn't hurt either. He knew how to avoid certain risks for the company, and he knew all the loopholes in the fine print of the contract, there to protect the company's money.

He had saved the company thousands by getting them good settlements when things like this came up and this particular case had been no exception. They had grudgingly paid the doctor one half of what he wanted, and they had settled out of court. Neither wanted to have the matter drawn out for months, which it surely would have been.

Jerry was thinking how glad he was that they had moved to North Carolina for a fresh start when he heard Kenny's car pull up into his circular driveway.

And now look at us, he thought. *The problems we had are nothing to the problems we have now.*

He watched Kenny scrape the snow off his windshield, angry that he didn't just come on in. Jerry was glad they had been fired. But not Kenny. He still fumed about it whenever it came up, and he had made sure it would be a part of their lives. Kenny had leverage over Browning if he ever needed it, and he was itching to use it "when the time is right."

Jerry had stepped in to help the company settle the suit with Dr. Leonard. He had shown, on paper, how they had offered the good doctor several payment options, none of which Dr. Leonard had fully been made aware of. Kenny did gloss over payments options but convinced the doctor that payment in full would be best as it would be "one less thing hanging over your head and you won't be strapped with all the interest."

Jerry had signed an affidavit as an eyewitness that Kenny had not misled the doctor. He had even stated, "We both felt sorry for the doc. We discussed his bad break, his wife dying and all, and sincerely hoped that he would enjoy his timeshare, as a means of moving on."

Once again, the mega vacation company won, at least in the fact that their image was protected. That's what counted the most. Each side had walked away somewhat satisfied, and no one had to go to court.

"A public court case could have really hurt out image," Rick had exclaimed at their going-away party.

Jerry smiled as he remembered that party.

"Going-away party," Jerry muttered to himself, getting angrier and angrier at Kenny, who was leaning against his car, talking on his cell phone. *Who the hell was he talking to?* Jerry wondered.

Rick Browning had made it look like he was doing them a favor by letting them retire early. Rick had explained that it was "best for everyone concerned" that he and Kenny does not stay with the company. "After all," he had said, "Kenny was indeed guilty of not honoring the three-day cancellation policy," even though that kind of thing happened all the time. And Jerry had been let go because Rick Browning had decided it was "time to downsize, my friend. I really can't afford you anymore."

Jerry had actually been glad. He couldn't have stayed there without Kenny.

The money, however, was a joke because Rick was a millionaire. Shortly after their retirement party, Rick had filed a suit against the two of them, just in case.

"Son of a bitch," Jerry had said when Kenny told him. Kenny had just smiled and reminded him of what happened at their going-away party. That party had given the leverage Jerry kept referring to.

"We'll blackmail him, Jerry. He'll drop the suit." And he had done just that but not because Jerry had kept copies of all the fraud he had committed to Rick. Kenny had concocted a much better plan, and it had worked. Browning had given them both glowing references when they moved.

Jerry missed the money he was making at the time-share company, but money wasn't everything to him the way it was for Kenny. Jerry loved having his own accounting business, and he was happy with work anyway. But the career move for Kenny wasn't so pleasant.

Kenny had previously worked as an attorney with a well-known law firm in Asheville, North Carolina. His father had started the firm years ago and was the lead attorney. He had even written a book about criminal law.

Kenny was just a mediocre attorney, but he was making good money. When he gave up his partnership in the law practice to go with Window to Your Dreams however, he had tripled his income, which pleased his father but made enemies of his former law partners.

Being at the firm again really bothered Kenny. He knew he was resented by his partners. He knew they were only "playing nice with me" because of his father. Kenny's father was actually a nice guy. Jerry admired him, but Kenny hated being under his thumb all the time. He hated working for him, period. And it was taking its toll. Kenny was drinking heavily again and on a regular basis, not just weekends.

Jerry looked out the front window and saw that Kenny was still on his cell phone. He was smiling. Jerry's jaw was clenched. He again wondered who it was on the phone that was keeping Kenny from coming in to console him. He wanted to trust Kenny, but it was hard to do so. He knew Kenny would never love him the way he loved Kenny. It used to be enough to be with him. Now he wasn't so sure, but he knew Kenny would help him. He always had, and he was his only family as far as Jerry was concerned.

"Who the hell is he talking to?" Jerry threw a can of beer toward the front door. He watched the beer splatter all over the door and down into the carpet. And Kenny was still smiling. Jerry knew Kenny would come in when he was good and ready and not a moment before. "Kenny, give me a break."

Jerry was feeling like he was going to cry. He was angry, but mostly sad. "We could have had such a good life." Jerry remembered when he had opened his own accounting services with financial help from Kenny. Jerry had been so proud and so thankful. He would always feel beholden to Kenny for all the financial help he'd given him.

Even now, Jerry vacillated between feeling angry and feeling sad. He realized that he never felt angry at Kenny for very long. At first he thought it was he loved Kenny so much. Then he realized it was much more than that. He felt guilty every time he got mad at Kenny. A part of him would always remind him, "You'd be nothing without Kenny." And that part kept him humbled and in Kenny's debt. He was satisfied with what he had money-wise and felt a personal sense of pride as well.

Kenny may have helped him start the business, *But I'm the one who's been a tremendous success at what I do*, Jerry thought.

Kenny had been unusually sad the last few days. The last time he was at Jerry's, he had plopped onto Jerry's sofa and cried like a baby. He had told Jerry that he was "sadder than I've ever been in my life" and "I've lost everything that ever mattered to me." Jerry had felt sorry for him at first, but as he listened to Kenny cry, he became more and more resentful.

He had slurred his words, but it was clear to Jerry what Kenny was referring to. He was talking about his precious little girl. He talked about how the nights with Libby had grown less and less over the years and how he had not gotten to spend enough nights in his daughter's bed before he gave her to Jerry. Jerry had wanted to punch him. Instead, he had just held him and let him cry it all out.

"It was good while it lasted," Kenny had murmured before falling off to sleep. Jerry remembered Kenny using the same exact words when Jerry had refused to share Libby after they were married. They had shaken hands, and Kenny had slapped him on the back, saying, "Okay, my friend. She's all yours. It was good while it lasted."

Kenny was really missing his time with Libby. That was clear to Jerry.

But I'm everything Kenny needs, Jerry had thought. *Why can't he see that? Why doesn't he want to see that?*

Kenny had cried as Jerry held him in his arms. "She started staying overnight with her friends way more than she should have been allowed and I told Norma just that." Kenny had gone on, drunk as a skunk at this point. He talked about how he needed to cuddle with his baby girl. It always made him feel better he said.

It made Jerry sick to hear Kenny crying in his sleep about losing Libby. *Does he love me at all?* he had wondered as he had helped Kenny into bed before turning to cry into his own pillow. Jerry had laid there for hours before falling asleep.

Kenny was talking like he was sorry he had given Libby to him. It made Jerry sad, and he wondered if he should have shared her with Kenny after all. In the end though it didn't matter because neither of them had her. And besides, Kenny was so drunk he wouldn't even remember saying all those things by the next morning, and sure enough, he didn't even mention it. Of course, Jerry didn't either.

Jerry remembered meeting Libby like it was yesterday. Her mother had not liked him. She hadn't known the kind of connection that Kenny and Jerry shared, but she didn't trust Jerry not even from the beginning. She knew that he drank too much. She knew there was more to their friendship than Kenny had let on, but she didn't know they were lovers. He was pretty sure about that. He and Kenny were very discreet.

Jerry and Kenny attended the same Sexaholics Anonymous meeting. Jerry remembered back to the night when Norma had come to pick Kenny up. She had seen Jerry and Kenny talking together. She didn't mention it at the barbeque, so Jerry was pretty sure she had forgotten him.

Norma had been attending Al-Anon meeting next door and had come to pick Kenny up. She had observed the pick-ups that were taking place after the Sexaholics meetings, and it had angered her. She had said something about it.

"Thirteenth stepping," she had shouted from her car.

She had referred to the Sexaholics meetings as a meet market as she gunned the motor and told Kenny that she needed to get home now! Jerry had been surprised to see Kenny laugh and walk slowly to the car. He felt sorry for Norma. He knew Kenny had beaten Norma up before.

Kenny had just bragged to the group how loyal Norma was to him. "Even when she makes me hit her, she doesn't complain. I think she realizes that she aggravated me to no end."

It had embarrassed Kenny when Norma had yelled at him. Jerry knew he would probably knock her around when they got home. Kenny had indeed been furious but had turned it around to make the scene gain him sympathy from his peers.

"See what I have to put up with?" Kenny had shrugged his shoulders and walked to Norma's car. At the next meeting, he informed the group that "she got a real tongue lashing on the way home, but I refrained from hitting her."

Jerry doubted very seriously that Kenny was telling the truth, but Jerry praised him for his restraint along with the rest of the group.

Norma had Kenny by the short hairs, even though he had a tight grip on her as well, the group had all agreed. It was one of those group conscience moments so obvious to everyone except Kenny. The group did try to discourage Kenny from being abusive to Norma.

He had shrugged more than once at their meetings when he was talking about everything he had to put up with, saying, "You do what you have to do to inherit all that money."

The group had just laughed but didn't pursue it. Everyone knew that Kenny's wife's mother owned half of Cashiers. And Rick Browning's family owned the other half.

Yes, it had been quite a surprise to them to find out that Rick Browning's father lived in Cashiers, North Carolina! They just hoped Kenny would stay out of their way.

Jerry resented the hold Norma had on Kenny though. It made him sick that Kenny would care that much about money instead of following his heart and going away somewhere to marry Jerry.

They had talked about it, about how Jerry wanted to settle down to the kind of life they were both meant to have with each other! Jerry had showed him all the states that now supported gay marriage. But Kenny wouldn't budge.

Jerry knew it would never happen. Norma's family's money won out every time. Kenny wanted that money. He was obsessed about it and had promised Jerry that if he didn't make waves related to his marriage to Norma, he would share that wealth with him. He had kept his promise. Because of his generosity, and that fact that Jerry was afraid of losing him, Jerry didn't complain.

He just let his own dreams fade away, deciding to take what he could get. They called him codependent in his AA group, but Jerry didn't care. The AA group actually worked the steps. It wasn't a bad group. He never mentioned Kenny by name, of course, but he did share with the group his sadness over the fact that his lover of several years would not commit and refused to come out of the closet.

Kenny came to that group occasionally, and when he did, you could see the anger on his face whenever Jerry mentioned his lover who would not commit.

Jerry did everything Kenny asked him to do, but he wasn't going to lie at his recovery meetings. He promised he would never expose Kenny as his lover, but that was the extent of his promises.

He wanted to get sober. He really did. He knew it would be hard to stay sober if he stayed with Kenny because he drank every time he was with Kenny.

"One day," Jerry would say to himself when Kenny wasn't around, "one day I'm going to get sober and stay sober."

It was something he held on to. He knew he needed to start making decisions that would help him to get sober and stay sober. He needed to think about what would make him happy, but he just couldn't bring himself to picture a life without Kenny in it, so most of his decisions were made in an effort to please Kenny.

"I even married your daughter, Kenny. What more do you want?" Jerry was crying now.

Kenny had been pleased when Jerry decided he would marry Libby but had been upset when Jerry had told him he didn't want to share her. Truth was, Jerry couldn't bear to think of Kenny with Libby.

It appeased Kenny for a while, but he was already back to drinking more and more. Jerry knew it was because of Libby! But what could he do? He wished with all his heart that he hadn't married Libby.

She would have eventually moved out of Kenny's life for good, and they would have eventually run off together.

"All these what-ifs," Jerry growled as he grabbed his shoes and started toward the front door. "No more time for what-ifs! We have to deal with the here and now." Jerry opened the front door. Kenny had walked around to the side of the house. "What the hell?" Jerry knew they were not exclusive, but this was his time and he was going to make sure Kenny knew it. "I know there are others," Jerry fumed as he sat down on the bench and put his shoes on.

They had decided long ago they would have an open relationship, or rather Kenny had decided it for them.

"But not in my driveway," Jerry seethed as he walked toward Kenny.

Kenny had walked all the way around the house and was sitting in Jerry's swing on the back patio.

Kenny knew Jerry was afraid he'd leave him. Jerry convinced himself that he couldn't stand it if Kenny left him. It wasn't just the way Kenny had taken care of him for so long financially. To Jerry, theirs was the kind of love that could have lasted a lifetime, at least his was toward Kenny. It would work if Kenny wanted it as much as Jerry did. But Kenny had wanted to try married life.

Well, that didn't work out well, did it? Jerry was thinking. *What if I have been more insistent? Maybe he would have married me instead?* Jerry mused, as if to clear his thoughts, then rubbed his hand through his thick, curly black hair. He was so angry he would have hit Kenny, had Kenny not turned around and handed him the pizza and beer Jerry had asked him to bring.

Then Kenny hugged him, and Jerry's anger melted. He was once again so grateful to have him.

"How did my life get so screwed up?" Jerry was crying into Kenny's chest, really sobbing his heart out. Within minutes he had already forgotten how angry he was with Kenny for sitting out in his driveway for so long on that damned cell phone. He was here now, and he would make everything better. He always did.

"Tell me all about it...later," Kenny had said and held Jerry an hour and just let him cry. An hour later, they were still in the swing, eating the cold pizza and drinking beer. It was nice.

Jerry was telling him all about getting buzzed at the corner bar, swerving on the ice, and hitting the man walking alone in the dark. He told him about hitting Libby with the baseball bat a few months back. He could see Kenny tense up. Although he hit Norma, Kenny had never laid a hand on his precious daughter, well, not the physical abuse he dealt with Norma.

"I lost it, Kenny. I just lost it. I really wanted her to have a boy. I really wanted to be a good daddy, better than my old man. I wanted that chance, but with a boy not a girl. I was really pissed about that, really pissed, Kenny. And today she said she wanted a divorce, so I punched her in the stomach. I knew you'd be upset about that. I didn't even think, Kenny. It just happened. You gotta believe me." Jerry was talking so fast. He could hardly catch his breath. And he was afraid of what Kenny might do to him for beating up Libby. But he had to get it all out, so he continued, "Why the hell did that doctor have to be Libby's hero? Hasn't he caused enough problems for us?" Jerry was crying again. "Kenny, they're going to find out it was me. They're going to come after me."

"Slow down, buddy." Kenny stroked Jerry's back. "The priest is going to live. I heard it on the radio coming over. And you said Libby was done with you, so let her go."

His tightened jaw did not go unnoticed. Jerry became angry that even now Kenny cared more about Libby than he did about him. He got off the swing and started toward the door.

"Why should I let her leave me? And what about the doctor, Kenny? I hit him hard. He could be dead for all I know."

Ignoring the question he had asked regarding Libby, Kenny followed Jerry inside. He brought the pizza and beer in with him. He sat down next to Jerry and started rubbing his back again. He knew it calmed Jerry down when he was overwrought.

"You're covered there, buddy. You just say the guy was trying to break into your wife's car and you hit him over the head. He could have been a potential robber. You were trying to protect your wife if she was still in the car and your property if she weren't. You worry too much, my friend. You're making a mountain out of a molehill."

Kenny's minimizing the situation only made Jerry angrier.

He shouted, "This problem is not going away, Kenny. The tow truck driver told me that the man was just lying there when he picked up the car. He said he was alive but barely breathing. He recognized him as a doctor at Transylvania Hospital and had called 911."

Kenny thought for a minute and told Jerry, "You should have taken his identification, dummy."

Jerry hated it when Kenny called him dummy or loser. He did it a lot, just like Jerry's father used to do. Kenny always apologized though, unlike his father.

Jerry looked at Kenny and said, "Well, I didn't and that's that. The tow truck guy said he was the same doctor who saved Libby and her baby right after operating on the priest that I hit on Asheville Highway. I almost choked when he told me that, Kenny. I had already heard it from that chatty nurse at the hospital, but hearing it again, I almost punched the guy. Instead I paid him the money I owed him and let it go. Kenny, run away with me…tonight! Please, Kenny, if you love me, leave with me tonight."

Kenny didn't say anything. He just kept rubbing Jerry's back.

What Jerry hadn't told Kenny was that when he had stopped at that bar, he had picked someone up. The guy was half Jerry's age, just a kid, but he took the money and did what Jerry wanted him to do, right there in the bathroom stall. Jerry didn't even like it. It sickened him as most things he heard at SA, but after a meeting, he had it on his mind and decided to try it. Afterwards, he just wanted to go home.

Jerry hadn't cheated very often, except with Libby, of course. And Kenny didn't see that as cheating since he set the whole thing up. But it had been a while since he and Kenny had spent any quality time together, and it had sounded exciting when his SA peer had shared his last encounter in a bathroom stall.

Jerry had been sick with guilt. The boy couldn't have been more than fourteen or fifteen years old.

"Kenny, I have got to get my life together. I feel like I'm falling apart."

"We'll deal with it, Jerry, all of it. It'll work out." Kenny stroked Jerry's cheek. "You know I'm sorry for calling you a dummy, don't you, Jerry?"

"Yes," Jerry had replied. "I know you always are. I'm scared, Kenny. I'm really scared. What are we going to do?"

Kenny thought for a minute. He didn't want to let Jerry down. Jerry was a good man. Kenny knew that Jerry was in love with him, but Jerry was his friend and more like a son to him than a partner (a son with benefits). This wasn't going to change. He wanted to help him but wasn't sure what to do.

"Jerry, I know you're scared. But I promise you, we'll fix this, okay? You gotta believe me, buddy, and calm down."

CHAPTER 4

Norma cried all the way back to the house she had shared almost nineteen years with Kenny. She assumed he would be at the office. Quickly, she packed more of her clothes and took out the money she had hidden under the mattress, stuffing it into her overnight bag, the one she kept in the front hall closet for emergencies. Norma walked into Libby's old bedroom. She almost gagged as she pictured Kenny there, in bed with Libby.

"How could I not have known?" she asked herself as tears streamed down her face. "How could a mother not know?" She vaguely remembered Libby trying to tell her that something was happening with Daddy that she had not liked. It had been a long time ago, and she remembered her reaction. *I didn't even give her a chance,* she thought. *Somewhere deep inside I must have known. I must have.*

Norma made a mental note to schedule another appointment with Helen. She wondered how Helen could even stand to look at her, knowing what kind of failure she had been as a mother. It was as if Helen was right in the room with her smiling and reminding Norma that a part of her had failed Libby, only a part. Many parts of her had done an excellent job with Libby.

Helen was a kind and gentle woman, an expert in her field and extremely compassionate. Norma wished that her mother had been like Helen. *That's crazy,* she thought. *Helen is younger than I am.*

Then she remembered a session in which Helen had explained to her about transference, that sometimes she might transfer feelings she really had about her mother onto her therapist and that it was perfectly normal to do so. Between Helen and her recovery groups, Norma was pleased with the progress she was making.

Norma had spent six months attending Al-Anon before she switched to CODA, Codependents Anonymous. She had felt more comfortable with them. This particular CODA group had moved beyond blaming themselves for their spouse's addictions and any domestic violence. It was a strong group, mostly women, and they were all very spiritual in their approach to life and to their overall healing process. Norma breathed a silent thank you to God as she gathered the rest of her things and made her way to the door.

There was no perfect in this life, but her small group came close. Even in that group though, *There was room for human error*, Norma thought. She thought of Harvey, a man who had tried to pick up several of the women in the group. They finally confronted him together, telling him it was not okay to hit on them, that they were there to heal and hoped he was there for the same reason. He had apologized and thanked them for "keeping me on the straight and narrow." And since then he had really turned his energy toward self-healing.

Some members in the group still blamed their parents for their problems. Most, however, just talked about the consequences they had experienced for being raised by parents who didn't know how to parent.

The group's overall resolve was to turn the page and move into the next chapter of their lives. They were trying hard to accept personal responsibility for their own behaviors as well as embrace the privilege of making their own mistakes, as they knew they would continue to do.

The CODA members that Norma felt closest to had advised her about Helen, the licensed clinical social worker they had seen or were still seeing. Norma had seen Helen for only two months, exactly eight sessions, before she decided to leave Kenny. She was grateful that Helen hadn't tried to convince her to leave Kenny, nor had she judged her as a bad person for wanting to divorce her husband. Norma hadn't even told her mother yet. Truth was, she had dreaded her mother's reaction. But after seeing Libby this last time, Norma was ready.

Being able to see Helen had also helped Norma get to the point of being ready to tell Constance. During the sessions with Helen, Norma was able to finally distinguish between forgiveness and codependence and martyrdom. Unlike some of her peers at Al-Anon and CODA, Norma believed in forgiveness as a way or releasing all the anger, sadness, and fears that are associated with an injury, no matter how big or small. She believed in finding peace through release. She believed in releasing the injurer as well. No ties at all. That was the motto she preferred but realized, as in the case of her mother, that some ties are good to keep, even when you are extending forgiveness.

She thought Helen would certainly judge her for her need to forgive, even when the injurer didn't deserve it. Quite the contrary, Helen had understood Norma's need to forgive Kenny over and over again. She had not criticized her in any way and had actually helped Norma to see that she was losing herself, her own dreams, her own ability to live out God's purposes for her apart from her family if she didn't choose forgiveness.

Norma had needed to hear that. It was like a light bulb went off in her head. It gave her the energy and determination she needed to move on, from the ending of one chapter to the beginning of another. Norma loved the analogy of her life being a book with many chapters. Just the thought of it gave her hope that the next chapter could be a better one.

Some of the women had met in her Al-Anon group believed that forgiveness meant staying in their unhealthy and unsafe relationships. Norma did not and was ready to move on. She felt no regrets because she knew she had done her best. She was excited about learning who she really was and what she really wanted. She had such excitement for what lay ahead. A new chapter indeed.

As she drove to her hotel room, Norma recalled her last session with Helen. Helen, being a Christian therapist, was comforting. Norma had told her insurance company that it was important to find a Christian and preferably one who had experience in cognitive behavioral interventions, as Norma had been told that particular approach was very helpful in reframing experiences that otherwise seemed unbearable. She also remembered a scripture that said, "As a man (male and female) thinks in his heart, so is he (meaning male and female)." Norma was sure that she didn't want to keep thinking angry thought about Kenny and was hoping Helen could help her with that.

Helen had asked Norma to read Matthew 19:19, "Love your neighbor as yourself." Then she had asked Norma how she had done that. Norma had rattled off all her experiences as a volunteer, always putting Kenny's needs first, even if they were not congruent with her values. Then she stopped, smiled, and whispered, "Oh, you want examples of how I have loved myself as well, don't you?"

Helen had smiled back. "How have you loved yourself in all of this, Norma?"

"I haven't," Norma replied tearfully.

She had then surprised herself by admitting, "I haven't really known who I was and what I really wanted out of life until just recently. I just did whatever my mother thought was best or what Kenny thought was best. I thought that was being a good daughter and a good wife, but now I realize I couldn't love anyone until I knew how to love myself."

It had been the revelation she needed, that she was not a bad person for leaving Kenny. She was not a bad person for getting her hair cut into a bob. It was a style she had wanted since she was Libby's age. She was not a bad person for needing to cry a lot when she felt sad, angry, or afraid. Her mother had called her histrionic and weak whenever she had found her crying. Constance never cried, or at lease Norma had never heard her cry, not even at her father's funeral. Her mother had been so stoic that Norma had worried about her. Constance had all but shut down after her father died. She was like an empty shell, never showing any emotional at all. Norma wondered if her mother (and herself) would ever find happiness again.

Helen had helped Norma see that all her crying actually released poisonous toxins and kept Norma sane. And with Helen's assistance through a bibliotherapy assignment, she realized that if she didn't ask for what she wanted in life, she wasn't likely to get it (Oprah Winfrey, *O Magazine*, July 2014).

She was finally ready to love herself. First step was getting her hair cut. It was Norma's way of saying, "I am an adult. I can make my own choices now. And if I make mistakes, they are my mistakes." Norma had felt like a teenager when she told her hairdresser to cut her hair into a bob and "No, it isn't a mistake."

She knew she was not making a mistake by leaving Kenny. Even before she and Libby reconnected, Norma had already decided to leave Kenny because of the physical and emotional abuse. She just wanted it over much sooner now, knowing the truth about what he had been doing to his own daughter!

To Norma, staying with Kenny would have meant completely losing herself. She had made the decision after a CODA meeting. That month Norma had begun pouring herself into learning more about self-acceptance and self-love. She also wanted to learn how to distinguish between this very healthy trait and narcissistic egotism. She wanted to love herself and others too.

Helen had suggested Norma read *Divine Conspiracy* by Dallas Willard. The entire book had been profoundly insightful, especially a quote from St. Augustine of Hippo about how we "go abroad to wonder at the height of the mountain, at the huge waves of the seas, at the long courses of the rivers, or the vast compass of the oceans. We wonder at the circular motion of the stars; and yet we pass right by our very selves, without wondering at all."

Norma had been blown away with that one. Even remembering it now brought chill bumps to her arms and a flutter in her heart. She had been so impressed she began to study other early church fathers and books on forgiveness. She had always assumed she had forgiven her mother but realized she hadn't. She couldn't really forgive or even love anyone fully until she could forgive and love herself. "Dear God, please don't let me ever take myself for granted again."

Reading was bibliotherapy, per Helen, and Norma enjoyed the assignments immensely. Helen was diligent in follow through too. She had always asked Norma if she liked the reading assignments. She had also asked Norma what she liked the most and least about each one.

St. Augustine of Hippo was, by far, Norma's favorite. He also thought this call to "wonder" at our very selves was intended by God to be our special dilemma. Norma wondered why women, especially Christian women, have this intense need to focus on others. She also wondered how we distinguish between enough and too much. Norma had taken the question to Helen, as she trusted her twenty-plus-years experience and expertise. She also admired Helen's unbridled passion toward helping others to see how special they are and what a gift to the world each person is.

Helen had told her, "From a beggar in the street to the humility of St. Francis, to the CEO of a Fortune 500 company. I could go on and on, but I believe we are all hardwired to focus our energy towards others. It is God's plan for our own well-being. Yet, we have badly misinterpreted that hard wiring because of our selfishness." She went on, "There are times when all of us want to be liked so much that we inappropriately focus on others as a means to that end...being liked. It is selfish because we are doing it for the wrong reasons. Regardless of the reasons, serving is an important goal because it still helps the people who are being served, regardless of the motives.

God didn't plan for service to be one-sided though. Relationships are designed to be reciprocal. It is the reciprocity of relationships that makes them healthy. God hard wires us to focus on others as a means of being fulfilled...not just them, but us too. Win/win!" Helen had grown quiet then. She had taken Norma's hands and said, "Giving and receiving of one another's gifts is the ideal, but it doesn't always happen that way, does it, Norma?" Norma had been tearful. Helen had gone on. "And yet when we step out of the way, it all works together, the good, the bad and the ugly."

Norma marveled at how much Helen had helped her and was so glad that God had led Libby to her as well.

Helen had read Romans 8:28 to Norma during a session. She had helped Norma process all the conflicting emotions that were surging up inside her.

"None of our life experiences are for naught, Norma," she had said kindly. "God uses all our life experiences, all the different and sometimes conflicting parts of ourselves in union with the different and conflicting parts of others. We all have gifts to share, and we all have unmet needs that get in the way sometimes."

It was during that session that Norma made a conscious choice to be less judgmental. All our experiences, even those intended for evil, will bring about good eventually. God only asks us to believe that it will happen and to allow it to happen, in God's time though, which is not necessarily ours.

Helen had reminded Norma as she had walked out the door one day, "Norma, never forget that good can come from evil."

And now God had given them Cody!

Norma remembered the last Billy Graham Crusade she had watched. A woman named Ethyl Waters had been a soloist that night. Her voice was like an angel's. Her testimony had been powerful. She told the crowd that she was the product of rape.

"What was meant for evil, God turned around for good. I am living proof of that. Make no mistake."

Norma admired that woman greatly. Ms. Waters had refused to let her own life be squandered just because of how she got here.

"And don't you let that happen to you either, no matter what you are facing right now," the woman had said.

Hers had been a profoundly moving testimony, and many men and women were crying by the time she finished.

"Know that God has a plan for your life."

What a blessing to have heard her testimony. Norma had been so grateful that Kenny was out of town that night. He didn't like for Norma to watch Bill Graham on TV and would have really criticized her for going to the Crusade in Asheville.

She had gone with her mother. They had spent a wonderful weekend together. They shopped. They sat in the hot tub and actually talked. They discussed the message that Graham had preached, one of the few times they actually got below surface talk. They even indulged in eating at some of the out-of-the-way places they had seen the last time they had visited. Both women loved God, and Norma was so thankful that they could get below the surface when talking about their faith. She really believed that one day it would be their faith in God that would bring them closer together.

Norma had shared this belief with Helen. She had admitted that she thought her mother was afraid of God.

Helen had replied, "Even Jesus, at least a part of him, was afraid of God's plan for him. He wanted to escape the torture that lay ahead of him. He begged God to let the cup of death pass him by. Yet another part of him wanted so much to fulfill all the purposes for which he had been born. He was so tormented by the battle within, he sweated blood. Yet, Jesus knew that in order to fulfill his final life's purpose, he must choose crucifixion, which ultimately freed him from his earthly body and brought witness to all of us, that we too will be raised from the dead and have new bodies just like Christ." Helen went on to say, "Remember that Mary Magdalene thought he was the gardener when she first saw Jesus after the resurrection."

During that session, Helen had explained her view on all the martyrs and saints who were honored from many different religions, not just Christianity.

"We are all saints," she had said, "at least parts of us are. We were all made in God's image, and no matter how badly we or some-one else tried to mar that image, it can't be destroyed. That part of us, our spirit, is the saint within. And, in that respect, we are all saints. We just have conflicting parts."

That had been a hard session for Norma. Helen had always been kind yet never coddled Norma. She was very direct, exercising tough love when it was needed, as they talked about the crucifixions that need to take place in Norma's own life.

Helen had said, "Sounds like it might be time to crucify these fears that have kept you from being true to yourself. And perhaps you may decide to crucify your misguided attempts to please your mother when certain requests have not been in your best interests."

Norma had understood and had laughed. "They aren't going to rise again in three days, are they?"

Helen had smiled. "They will try to, Norma," she had said kindly. "I believe that because we all have these conflicting parts of ourselves, we are all at risk for codependency at any given time, depending on the external circumstances as well as the internal ones, such as which part of us is expressing her need the strongest. Knowledge is very powerful and wisdom even more so. You are making excellent progress in learning who you are and what you really want."

Norma had appreciated the compliment because she knew it was true. She had thought of her mother and realized there were parts of her mother in her and had marveled at the awareness that it was okay.

"Yes, I see now that all of us want to be accepted, to be good at something," she had told Helen.

Norma had processed and worked through painful memories where she hadn't felt loved by her mother. Helen had encouraged her to step back and look at which parts of her mother Norma may have been struggling with at those particularly painful times and then to "walk a mile in that part of your mother's shoes." It had been enlightening and an extremely helpful assignment.

Helen called it psychosynthesis. And through these visualizations, Norma was able to see her mother in a new light, a vulnerable human being who just wanted to be noticed, just wanted to be liked.

"That's why her status, her place in society, is so important to her," Norma had cried. "It wasn't that she hated me as much as it was her need to be accepted. And if I wasn't dressed a certain way, didn't date the right boys, or marry the right man, my life would reflect negatively on her and make her look bad."

That session had also been painful. "But that's so selfish," she had cried.

Yes, it is," Helen had agreed. "Codependency is very self-centered. We convince ourselves that it is other-centered, but it is not. Your desperate attempts to please your mother weren't any different from her desperate attempts to please her socialite friends, were they, Norma?"

"Was my mother still codependent after Daddy stopped drinking?" she had asked Helen. "I really don't remember Daddy as an alcoholic. He had stopped smoking and drinking. He quit cold turkey and loved bragging about that to everyone." She went on to explain, "I thought you had to be married to someone with an active addiction to be codependent."

Helen had smiled and reminded her about the many experts in the field that couldn't agree on what codependency was exactly, so she was not alone.

Norma remembered telling Helen about her first introduction to codependency. Norma had gone to an open AA meeting with Kenny. They were talking about the various experts on codependency.

Norma had left the meeting deeply confused. "None of these experts can agree on what codependency is," she had said to Kenny.

Kenny had just shrugged. He didn't care one way or the other. Being liked by his peers was more important to him than in sorting out the codependency issues he himself had. Norma had even accused him of being addicted to meetings and the friends he had there. He had attended three meetings a week for over fifteen years, and when Norma suggested he needed to broaden his social horizons by getting "out there and meet life on its own terms," Kenny had gotten physical and slapped her, telling her to live her own life and he would live his.

Norma had wished that she and Kenny could actually talk about what they were learning in their respected groups. But Kenny was not interested in using what they were learning as a means to grow closer to his wife.

Helen had called his behavior addictive. Norma had been confused. "Yes, I know he is an addict. That's why he goes to these groups."

But Helen had explained how some people in recovery get addicted to the groups themselves. "It is hard for some because if they get to a point they don't really need to attend as often as they once did, they feel disloyal to their group and it feels like they've relapsed. For these, the groups are their fix."

It made perfect sense to Norma, who had started out going to meetings twice a week and now attended only once a week. Her sponsor only attended once a month but kept in contact with Norma as often as she was needed.

Norma reflected on the session in which Helen described all the parts she had to sort out. Norma was now able to realize that Kenny too had many parts. It had been surprising to realize that many of the parts of Kenny that she didn't like were similar to the parts of her mother that she found distasteful, like wanting to be liked by everybody. A bibliotherapy assignment called *Getting the Love You Want* by Harville Hendrix had shed some light on this issue as well.

Her mother's need to be accepted was a priority, over and above her own child. It controlled here very decision, to the point that she couldn't bear thinking her own family might have skeletons in the closet.

"Oh my God!" Norma had winced as she realized that she did indeed have a small part of her mother in her as well as having been drawn to that part in Kenny. She thought of when she had completely blocked from her mind that anything wrong could be going on between her husband and her child.

"That would have reflected badly on me as a mother?" she had asked Helen.

"Maybe," Helen had said gently. "It also may have been hard to accept because if Kenny wanted Libby instead of you, what did that make you?"

Norma didn't respond. She just sat there, stunned.

"How do you feel about it now?" Helen had asked.

"Like I was a terrible mother," Norma had said. But then she was able to smile, because she got it. "I was just like my mother in that respect, and I didn't even realize it. Okay, I'm learning." She had hated to admit that she had married parts of her mother in Kenny.

Helen had explained, "We often marry parts of our parents. It is usually subconscious, but it is our way of working out unresolved issues with one or both of those parents. The theory behind that school of thought is Imago Relationship Theory. That's when Libby was assigned the book by Hendrix, even though the book was also prescribed for couples in therapy. But Helen thought the insight of marrying different parts of ourselves might be helpful to Norma, and it had.

Norma had been genuinely interested in all the insights she was gaining as a result of therapy and in attending the recovery meetings. She had been introduced to Daniel Goleman's emotional intelligence theory and was fascinated to learn that it was important to have a high EQ because even if you had a high IQ, if you didn't know how to manage your own emotions, the high IQ wouldn't serve you very well. Fascinating theory and absolutely true!

As a result, Norma had begun trying to better manage her emotions as well as her thoughts, and her behaviors often followed suit. She knew she would never be perfect, that she would indeed make more mistakes, but she was learning and that in itself gave her a tremendous feeling of self-love and empowerment.

Kenny, on the other hand, seemed to have given up on learning about his irrational thinking and codependent behaviors. He had continued his cheating and verbal and emotional abuse. Nothing had changed because Kenny wasn't interested in change. He just went to weekly confession, confessed his sins, said ten Hail Marys and five Our Fathers, and went right back out to sin the same sins again over and over. It made Norma sad to remember this but no longer bitter and unforgiving. She actually found herself feeling sorry for Kenny, not in a self-righteous manner, rather in a compassionate way.

Helen had encouraged Norma to talk about her sadness at CODA, which had proven very beneficial. Norma had discovered that one of the reasons she didn't like going to church anymore was because Kenny had embarrassed her at church and it had made her sick the way he abused the confessional. She had almost turned her back on her own faith, her beloved parish, the church she loved. She shared about a time when she and Kenny were both in line at the confessional. Kenny had looked at his watch, mentioned he was late for his Sexaholics Anonymous meeting, and had stepped out of line and left.

When Helen had asked Norma about the insights she had gained as a result of sharing this with her group, Norma admitted how much it hurt her to realize that Kenny even placed his relationship with God second when it came to choosing between confession and being late to a meeting! And she had admitted to the group that she didn't feel so embarrassed or judgmental when she stopped and realized what Kenny had done to his own faith, his own relationship to God.

"My CODA peers were gentle yet firm, calling me on it and encouraging me to get back involved in my parish. I have done that. And it has been good, cleansing." Norma shared her gratitude for Helen and for the CODA group. "I can be myself there and here," Norma had said. No condemnation. She had even admitted to Helen and to her CODA group that she had been in love with a priest and had made love with him the night before she married Kenny. Helen, as well as her group, had been kind, nonjudgmental.

They had returned to their discussion about Kenny's lack of interest in going to church, "except to make sure everyone knew he was an attorney, if they ever needed one."

Helen had told Norma, "There will always be those who hide behind religion or misuse their opportunity to find God. But, Norma, your life isn't really about what Kenny thinks about God or about church, is it?" Helen sure had a way of getting Norma back to the issue at hand.

It was in that same session that she had helped Norma sort out her confusion about how different authors approached the subject of codependency from very different viewpoints.

"All have merit," Helen had pointed out. "Take the good and leave the rest."

It had seemed so simple when Helen had said that.

Norma had laughed. "That's too easy."

Helen had laughed right back. "And what about easy is hard for you?"

CHAPTER 5

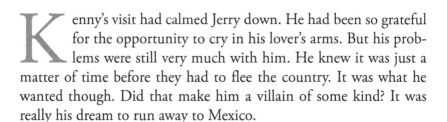

Kenny's visit had calmed Jerry down. He had been so grateful for the opportunity to cry in his lover's arms. But his problems were still very much with him. He knew it was just a matter of time before they had to flee the country. It was what he wanted though. Did that make him a villain of some kind? It was really his dream to run away to Mexico.

Jerry had seen pictures of Cancun, one of the few times he and Libby were at her grandmother's home before they got married. Their housekeeper, Maria, had shown them pictures of her with her sisters and brothers.

Jerry had actually been strongly attracted to one of Maria's brothers at one time. Miguel had flirted with him all afternoon. Kenny hadn't been there, just Jerry and Libby. Libby had spent a lot of time in the kitchen with her grandmother, mother, and Maria.

Jerry knew Miguel was interested, and Jerry had to fight the attraction he felt for him. But Jerry had already promised Kenny he would marry Libby, and at the time Jerry was sure that if he did this for Kenny, they would one day wind up together, so he hadn't pursued Jesus's attentive behavior.

He was surprised to be thinking of Miguel at a time like this. Jerry had gone down to the corner market for a pack of cigarettes.

He made the mistake of charging them. The cashier had recognized his name from the TV's local news. Jerry looked up at the TV, just as the cashier did. There was his picture, all over Channel 5. Before he knew what was happening, the cashier had notified the police and he had been arrested for assaulting Dr. Leonard. As far as he knew, that's all they had on him but he was sweating bullets, waiting for his phone call.

Here he was in the county jail with real criminals. He never thought of himself as a criminal, not even when he ran the priest over with his car and left the scene of the accident.

I'm not a bad person, he thought. *I've had the deck stacked against me all of my life. I've never had a break. But Kenny will get me out of this mess. He always gets me out of my messes.*

Jerry's father had abandoned him after his mother had died. He had abused him pretty badly before he just gave up on him. He didn't notice him much, unless Jerry made a mistake. Then Jerry got burned with cigarettes.

He thought of the cigarettes he was buying at the time of his arrest.

You'd think I would have given these horrible things up by now, he thought. *They've always been bad news for me.*

Having to live in an orphanage for a few years had not been a good life. They weren't mean to him. It had been hard on Jerry emotionally though, because being an orphan meant he didn't have a daddy or a mommy. He eventually did go into foster care, but his life hadn't gotten better.

In fact, it had gotten worse. His foster mother reminded him daily, "If you're not a good boy and pick that mess up, I'll send you right back to the streets." And his foster father? Jerry shook his head, as if to clear the memories.

But he had stayed in the foster home because he wanted to have a mother and a father. Jerry was determined to have a mother and a father, no matter how mean they were. It felt more normal than living in an orphanage.

So he had listened to his foster mother's daily verbal abuse and tried to be good. He had nightmares that he would be sent back to the streets, as she warned on at least a weekly basis if he forgot to brush his teeth or didn't comb his hair the right way or made bad grades in school. He had been terrified of her threat to send him back, to take away the little bit of normalcy he had.

His foster father was a real piece of work. He was always laughing and joking. Jerry initially thought he was going to be a fun daddy. But he was anything but fun the week Jerry had moved in with them.

It used to make Jerry sick, the way his foster father would make him sleep next to him without any clothes on. Then he started touching Jerry inappropriately. After that, it just got worse.

He learned how to do it right though. It was always the same. He would zip his pants up and slap Jerry on the back, saying, "Good boy, you're learning.

Jerry knew he had better learn because his biological father had not only burned him with cigarettes, he had beaten him black and blue when he did things incorrectly. This was before the school psychologist had made a formal complaint. That particular week Jerry's father had burned him with his cigarette butt when he came home from school too late. The psychologist had seen the crusted over spots on Jerry's arm the next day at school. She knew Jerry was being abused, but she couldn't ever prove it. That day she had immediately called child services.

Jerry had been taken out of the home and sent to the orphanage, pending an investigation. Then there was a court hearing. His father had talked to the judge. The judge had ordered counseling. Then Jerry went back to his father.

Jerry's father had been very convincing, saying that he had fabricated the whole thing and "it wasn't the first time," he told the judge. "I think he does these things to himself because he ain't been right since his mother died."

Jerry had paid dearly for all the trouble he had made for his father.

The next month, however, the school psychologist made another report, and Jerry had been removed for good. He didn't much care though because his father didn't really want him. He knew that. He had run away from the orphanage a few times but had always gone back. At least they didn't beat him there and didn't burn him with cigarettes. But it wasn't a real family, which Jerry wanted more than anything else in the world.

Jerry was in and out of foster homes, but no one wanted to adopt him, and he had finally run away from the last one. He could have put up with the threats from his foster mom, even the sexual favors to his foster dad, if they had ever talked about adoption. But when he had asked, they made it clear they didn't have plans to adopt him, just helping the state by giving him a place to live. When Jerry turned thirteen, he ran away.

"They won't adopt me," he had told himself. "Nobody will." He didn't want to go back to the orphanage this time. *No more foster parents. Nobody really wants me*, he thought and figured he would be better off on the streets.

It was hard at first. He was scared and hungry, and he cried a lot. After a few weeks of giving guys oral sex for food, he met a guy who asked him to move in. He said he would "love him like a son."

The guy owned a video store and had found Jerry sleeping in the bathroom when he opened up one morning. Jerry had let him buy him breakfast, and he hung around watching Rafael work. It was kind of fun, hanging out in a video store.

He decided to give it a try. He had his own room in the huge apartment. He was allowed to pick out any videos he wanted to watch and got them for free. Rafael fed him well. He didn't have to go to school, and best of all he wasn't beaten.

Rafael had even been angry when Jerry had told him what he was doing out on the streets at night.

"You could have been killed, kid," Rafael said one night as he pulled the covers up under Jerry's chin.

One night, about a month after Jerry had moved in, he was sitting cozily in a La-Z-Boy, blanket wrapped around him. He had a bowl of popcorn in his hands. He was happy, maybe for the first time in his life. He was watching one of his favorite movies when Rafael came in and picked Jerry up, sitting him on his lap.

"You're a good kid, Jerry." Rafael told him. "I want to show you how much I love you."

Jerry had said, "Okay."

Rafael did inappropriate things, but Jerry didn't mind. It was like the abuse from his foster father. Rafael rubbed Jerry's back the whole time. Jerry felt very special and "loved."

His foster father had never done that. Jerry was never the one getting the "favors," and his foster daddy got all the "favors." Even on the streets, it was always Jerry doing that or worse for some other man.

But this time it was Jerry who got to feel good. This kind of "loving" went on for about a week. Jerry enjoyed it.

"Not bad," he had said to himself. Truth was, he thought he'd died and gone to heaven.

Then one morning before Rafael went off to work, he told Jerry, "Hey, buddy how about you show me how much you love me."

Jerry was startled, but had said, "Sure."

He rubbed Jerry's back the whole time. At first Jerry had flashbacks to his foster father. But he quickly buried them. "It isn't the same thing," he told himself. "Rafael loves me." Afterwards, they hugged and Rafael was off to work. After that morning, this kind of "loving" continued on a regular basis. At least it was reciprocal with Raphael.

"A mutual loving," Jerry told himself.

Jerry convinced himself life was good. After all, their "loving" was in the context of a real relationship, not forced like it was at his foster home or on the streets. And Rafael was so good to him. He had even bought him his own DVD player and TV for his room. Rafael promised he would adopt Jerry "as soon as I have the money." Jerry could hardly believe his ears. It was all he had ever wanted—a real father.

He lived with Rafael for four years. He was happy. Then one day, shortly after they had celebrated Jerry's seventeenth birthday, Rafael didn't come home from work. Jerry became frightened because

Rafael always called him when he was late. Jerry had a little anxiety every day, but it subsided when Rafael got home.

Jerry had turned on the television and tried to find a good movie to keep him company and get his mind off his fears. He flipped through the channels, to a news station, and saw a picture of Rafael flashing on the screen. He had been murdered during a robbery at the video store. The store's video camera had caught it on tape. Jerry was numb at first. He sat in the same position for hours, afraid to move. He cried until there were no more tears.

He stayed at Rafael's apartment until the food ran out and all the cash Rafael had hidden was gone. He avoided the landlord in the process. Sooner or later he would find out Jerry was living by himself and call child services. Jerry was seventeen now but still underage to live alone.

Eventually, he went back to the streets and became a prostitute once again. He didn't like everything he was asked to do and was beaten up occasionally, but the money was good, and he did okay.

After a year though, when he turned eighteen, Jerry allowed himself to think about Rafael again. He grieved the loss of his best friend, the only one in the world who really loved him. Thinking about his life with Rafael, Jerry had wondered if he might ever find someone to love him again. That's when he had decided to go to a Sexaholics Anonymous meeting. He had seen the people coming in and out of the building across the street from where he picked up most of his "clients" and had even talked to a couple of the men, one of whom suggested Jerry "join them at a meeting sometime."

Jerry decided to take him up on it, and that's when he got to know Kenny. Kenny was an older man, an attorney. Jerry liked the group at first. He got very aroused, listening to the stories these men and women told, stories about their forbidden sex. He was learning about new places to go for anonymous sex and hearing about all kinds of ways to have sex with people who went there were really twisted.

"But, hey, to each his own," Jerry would remind himself.

Jerry really didn't think these particular meetings were helping anyone who went to get "sober" though, as most all of them were just screwing each other, some openly, some sneaking around like it was a crime.

"I guess it is a crime, if you think it's wrong," Jerry had told Kenny one night.

After a few meetings, Kenny had asked Jerry if he wanted to go get a coffee after the meeting. Jerry had said yes. After a while Kenny took him under his wing, paying for him to get his GED, setting him up in a small studio apartment, and enrolling him in college. It was a good life once again.

Kenny actually adopted Jerry, or at least he showed Jerry some papers that said he had adopted him. Jerry was so excited, he never questioned Kenny. He paid for Jerry's entire education all the way through graduate school and then law school. He double majored in accounting and business law. It had been a pleasant surprise to Jerry to find out that he was actually very intelligent. He missed Rafael but was beginning to love Kenny very much.

Kenny told Jerry he was "the son I always wanted" and "the best lover I have ever had." Their arrangement went on for several years. They worked together at a large time-share company and had some wonderful years together. Then they got fired from there and moved together from Florida to North Carolina. Things were good.

Then one day. Kenny told him he was getting married.

"You can't ever tell her about us, Jerry. She would never understand. Her old lady is rich, and one day you will inherit your share from us. But you have to keep your mouth shut, or you'll ruin everything. I'm telling you for your own good, okay?"

Jerry had nodded.

Kenny was wealthy in his own right. He was the star attorney at his father's firm. When his grandfather had died, he had left his law firm to Kenny's father, who would one day leave it to Kenny, who would bring Jerry on board as the firm's CPA. John had been a good grandfather to Jerry, even though he didn't know the whole story about Jerry's relationship to Kenny. He was just a kind old man who loved Kenny's father and Kenny very much. It had been Kenny's mother that Kenny hated. Jerry hated her too.

She had been homophobic since before Kenny was born, and Kenny knew he could never come out as long as she was alive. But he had promised Jerry, "As soon as she's six feet under, Jerry. Meanwhile, we play the game."

Jerry knew that Kenny had begun seeing women a year or so before he married Norma. He didn't mind at first. Kenny still loved him. He had been staying with Jerry less and less though, and it had worried Jerry. Kenny was always talking about how he wanted a normal life. To Kenny, a normal life was having a "heterosexual life with wife and kids." So it finally happened. He had met the one he was going to marry, and Kenny wanted Jerry to be glad for him.

Kenny told Jerry he had met Norma at a friend's house. The friend was a former sales director at the same time-share company he and Jerry had worked, Window to Your Dreams, in Orlando, Florida. Norma's uncle was good friends with Rick Browning, the CEO of the company.

"I want to marry her, Jerry, which means I can't see you as much. But I won't forget you. I'll find a place for you in the family, I promise. Just give me time."

Jerry wished him well. What else could he do? He didn't like it though, not at all.

Norma and Kenny had a lavish wedding, as Kenny called it, in Cashiers, North Carolina. Kenny's father had been proud of Kenny, and his mother was over the moon about Norma. She had made it clear to Kenny that she was expecting a grandchild as soon as possible. Jerry was not invited to the wedding but read all about it in the newspapers. Norma's parents were high society, as Kenny was fond of saying. Norma got pregnant the night they were married and had a baby girl.

Kenny was doing very well financially. He missed the excitement they had when they worked at Window to Your Dreams, and he missed Jerry. He said he felt torn between "the excitement you and I have had" and the lure of Norma's family's money. Jerry knew Kenny missed his job in Orlando. He had often bragged to Jerry about sticking it to the old geezers.

He did still visit Jerry once a week. "Business trips," he would tell Norma, and he and Kenny would laugh and reminisce over beer and pizza and sleeping late together. Jerry didn't complain. He was afraid Kenny would leave him entirely if he did.

Kenny loved being a father. Libby was a cute baby with her blond hair and blue eyes. Kenny was always showing Jerry photos of her. Jerry remembered thinking, *She doesn't look a thing like you, Kenny.*

Kenny was Puerto Rican and dark-skinned, but Jerry never said anything out loud because he could tell it would make Kenny mad. He obviously loved his little girl.

The kid had Kenny wrapped around her little finger, and Jerry actually became jealous of her at one point. As she grew, Libby began spending more and more time with her father and Kenny was spending less and less time with Jerry.

He and Kenny had agreed, even before Kenny married Norma, that they would have an open relationship, which meant that either of them could have sex with anyone else they might be attracted to, in or out of the meetings they attended. So far Jerry had not indulged. He was fiercely loyal to Kenny. He didn't like cheating and was surprised that Kenny wanted to cheat—on him or Norma.

As time went by, Jerry wasn't afraid Kenny would leave him. He had been faithful to his word. He had promised that he would always protect Jerry, and he had. They continued to keep their relationship a secret however, and that continued to bother Jerry. He didn't mind being gay. He wanted to shout it from the rooftops, "It's who I am," and wished that Kenny wasn't so uptight about it. He didn't blame Kenny though. He blamed Kenny's mother.

"If she wouldn't go nuts and disown him, Kenny would have married me years ago," Jerry told himself as he waited for Kenny to post bail. *Surely, he is on the way*, Jerry thought.

Kenny's daughter Libby was nine years old when Jerry noticed Kenny hardly came to see him at all. Libby had blossomed into a "beautiful little girl," Kenny told Jerry. He had bragged about her to the point that Jerry thought he would puke if he heard her name one more time.

What he didn't know was that Kenny had begun really abusing this beautiful little girl. Kenny didn't tell him because he knew Jerry was jealous of the time he spent with Libby. But Kenny soothed his own conscience by telling himself, "I just can't help it. She is just too pretty to ignore. And she is mine after all."

Libby didn't like it at first. Kenny knew that. But he convinced himself she would in time. After all, it took him years to enjoy sex with women, but he did now. It was nice to have variety, he told himself. And now this sweet little girl, his own flesh.

There was "something exciting about it all," Kenny had told Jerry.

It made Jerry sick just to think about it. "It's wrong, just wrong," he told himself over and over again, but he never told Kenny. Instead, he listened over and over again to the stories about Daddy's little girl, as Jerry was so fond of calling Libby.

He still saw Jerry, but the visits, rare as they were, became shorter and shorter. Kenny became obsessed with Libby. He was a "good father," he told Jerry more than once. "That means spending time with your kid." He took her on camping trips. He took her sailing. He always took her side when she and her mother had an argument. Jerry hated it. He actually felt sorry for Libby, and at times he hated Kenny. "He's all screwed up in the head," Jerry would tell himself.

Kenny had made sure that Libby wouldn't tell anyone. He hadn't wanted to scare her, but he told her if she ever said anything to anyone, especially her mother, Norma would hate her and probably want to get rid of her. It had been enough to scare the child into silence. Jerry remembered how scared he was as a kid getting sexually abused by the people who were supposed to protect him.

As Jerry lay there on the cot of this dingy jail he had begun calling the pit of hell, Kenny finally walked in with one of the guards.

"You're getting out of here, buddy." Kenny had paid Jerry's bail. It had been $250,000. "They arrested you for beating up Dr. Leonard, Jerry, but they say you might have hit that priest as well. That's why the bail was so high. They say you are a flight risk."

Kenny told him as they were leaving, "You still have the arraignment to get through, Jerry. But we will figure out a way to wash all of this away."

Kenny was always so optimistic. It was one thing Jerry had admired about him. But this time he didn't believe his dear friend.

Yes, they had moved to North Carolina after the terrible episode at the time-share company, and yes, life was easier. But Kenny remained obsessed with his daughter, so Jerry was always uncertain, always wondering, *Will he get tired of me altogether?* Now would be the time.

As they walked out, Jerry started crying. "Kenny, that doctor I hit over the head, he's getting better every day! I don't know what the big deal is with him." He didn't even give Kenny a chance to answer before he went on, "And the priest? Dr. Leonard saved his life as well as Libby's, but he too is going to live. They are both going to be fine. But it doesn't matter, they were going to put me away, Kenny. We have to leave town before the arraignment."

Kenny just smiled in the way he always did when he was sure of himself, and this was no exception.

"I paid that good doctor a visit yesterday, Jerry. I told him he'd better stay away from Libby. I also told him that I knew he had you arrested for assault. I think he was pretty shaken up when I left." He patted Jerry's back.

Jerry became hopeful. "Are you sure, Kenny?"

Kenny assured him, "We don't have to worry about the doctor, Jerry. I made it clear that he didn't know what a real beating was like, and he wouldn't get up from the next one if he didn't leave you and Libby alone."

"God, I hope you are right, Kenny. I hope you are right."

Kenny tried to soothe Jerry's fears. He did care about the boy, well, the young man Jerry had become. He was still a kid when Kenny had first taken him in. Now he is a handsome and successful young man. Kenny felt a sense of pride that he had been a part of that.

Jerry felt a need to defend himself. "Kenny, you gotta know I didn't know who Dr. Leonard was at first. Didn't know he was the same guy I hit over the head at Libby's car that night. Not that it would have mattered. When I saw him smiling at Libby and her baby the day they were released from the hospital, I lost it. As soon as he left her room, I grabbed his coat and threw him into what I thought was an empty room, right next to hers. Punching him in the stomach was easy. But I turned and looked at the bed he had fallen onto after I punched him and thought I'd have a stroke. I couldn't believe my eyes when I saw that priest lying there. When he recognized me, I panicked. He called for the nurse, telling her that his assailant, the man who had hit him and left him for dead was right there in his room. What the hell? I just ran. Kenny, I just ran." Jerry rubbed his hand through his thick black hair. "I never meant for him to see me, but he did. I wanted to make sure he was still breathing when I left, and he was, Kenny. There wasn't a light on anywhere, just the moon, but he saw me."

He was talking a mile a minute. Kenny could tell he was agitated and knew that Jerry would work himself up into a panic attack if he didn't calm him down. Jerry had experienced panic attacks before, but Kenny had always helped him.

"I ran, but they caught me anyway because I had to have those stupid cigarettes. Yes, I'm charged with assault on the good doctor and won't be long before they confirm it was me in the hit and run! Thanks for putting up my bail, Kenny, but we have got to get out of town. I mean it this time, Kenny."

Jerry was sobbing uncontrollably. Kenny wasn't sure what to do. He took him to a motel down the street and just held him and let his cry. Now wasn't the time for sex and to be quite honest, he didn't even want it. He did care about Jerry and was frightened for him. He had never seen him so worked up.

"Wait a minute, Jerry," Kenny said. "I have an idea. I know where we can get a gun, one that can't be traced back to us. It belongs to Norma's late father. Norma's mother is always out on Tuesdays, and it is the maid's day off. I know exactly where the gun is. Let's go and get it. It shouldn't be hard."

"And just how are we going to get in," Jerry asked in astonishment. He knew Kenny was right though. They not only had the law after Jerry, but Kenny had the CEO of Window to Your Dreams after him, probably for some money they had embezzled from the company before they were fired or, worse, he was still angry over the video they took of Rick's indiscretion at their retirement party. Rick had sued both of them, but Jerry thought that was all over with.

Kenny was still talking. "He used to keep the gun in his desk drawer, per Norma. It always scared her, knowing it was there. It will be easy, Jerry, and nobody will ever know that we took it. Hell, they will probably blame the maid, so let's go."

They walked to Kenny's car, and as they drove, they laid out their plan. Jerry's biological father had walked back into Jerry's life a year before. Jerry had actually been afraid of him when he first saw him after all those years.

But Bobby had told Jerry he was "a changed man" and he wanted to "get to know my son under better circumstances." He had stopped drinking, which was a big surprise to Jerry. He was a taxi driver and owned his own taxi service.

Jerry told Kenny he felt sure his old man would let them use one of his drivers to take the over to Norma's mother's house. They would have him wait until they got the gun. They wouldn't tell him what they were planning, of course, just have him wait with the engine running.

"The kid is at day care," Kenny said. He didn't even think of her as his granddaughter, and Jerry barely looked at her the last time he was in Libby's hospital room. "Norma is now working for Dr. Leonard as his receptionist. Libby is in class. She is finishing up her degree in clinical social work. Can you believe it?" Jerry noticed his friend's jaw tighten.

Kenny was bitter that he no longer had control over Libby. And he hadn't seemed to care at all that she had left Jerry. That bothered Jerry, but what was he to do? He did wonder how Kenny knew so much about Libby and Norma when he hadn't seen them in months!

The plan to get the gun went along smoothly, at least in getting the taxi driver to take them. What they hadn't planned on, however, was the housekeeper giving up her day off to be there at the Galyon home to coordinate the renovations they were doing on the mansion.

She had done so for several weeks, at least while Constance was with her poker group. It was the least she could do for this family who had been so good to her. She opened the door when she saw the taxi pull up outside the mansion. She was upset to see Kenny and Jerry step out of the taxi. She screamed at them in Spanish and told them they had to leave. They rushed past her, knocking her down, and headed into the study.

The gun was right where Kenny said it would be. Maria had come back inside and had picked up the phone and was calling the police. Before he even knew what he was doing, Jerry's finger was on the trigger. He aimed the gun at Maria and shot her.

As the blood began to pool around her body, Kenny yelled at Jerry, "Are you crazy?"

Jerry was completely out of control. "It just happened, Kenny. My mind flashed back to the day Rafael was shot. I saw the picture on TV, Kenny, from the camera at the video store. I saw Rafael, but I shot the maid. Rafael's death really messed with my mind, Kenny. Anyway, the gun just went off. I didn't mean to kill her."

Kenny just shook his head. Jerry had an excuse for everything. "Well, Jerry, you did shoot her. You killed her. Now let's get out of here."

They ran out the front door and was stopped by Norma's mother, whose car had just pulled up.

"I don't know what you boys are doing here, but if I ever see you here or around my family again, I promise you I will hire a professional to tear you from limb to limb. Do you understand? I have enough money to make sure you are both ruined for the rest of your life. And I won't hesitate to use it. Now get out."

They ran to their own taxi and sped away. Jerry had wanted to kill her too, but Kenny had convinced him that she wouldn't say anything.

"That old bitch would rather die than let anyone know what happened here today," he had told Jerry. "Her reputation means far more to her than what you did to her housekeeper."

Kenny was convinced they were safe from Constance. Now they just had to figure out a way to be safe, period. Jerry was right. They had to get away. Now more than ever. That was for sure. But they needed money to do that, and that bitch had plenty of money. They would find a way to help her get rid of a few million, and he and Jerry would start all over again, somewhere else.

Kenny stayed with Jerry that night. The next morning they awoke to dear old Grandmother being interviewed on television. Kenny sat up and rubbed his eyes. He couldn't believe what he was hearing.

"It was heart-wrenching," she was saying. "I walked in. I found Maria on the floor and my husband's gun was missing. I still can't believe it." Constance Galyon was sobbing on local TV!

"What the hell? I'm telling you, Jerry. That old broad would never have told a soul about this before. But now that she had her precious daughter, her granddaughter, and now her great-grand-daughter all living with her, she's a changed woman." Kenny was so agitated, he spilled last night's beer all over the carpet.

"What are we going to do, Kenny?" Jerry was up now and pulling on his clothes. He was wondering again how Kenny knew so much about where Libby and her mother lived and what they were doing with their lives.

They hadn't heard the entire interview, so they didn't know at that point whether she had mentioned seeing them or not.

"Settle down, Jerry. Haven't I always made things okay for you? I am thinking of a fantastic way to get back at all of them, Jerry. We will kidnap the kid. Am I good or what?"

"Who wants to be saddled with a toddler?" Jerry complained.

"Think about it, my friend. Your daughter is our ticket out of here. The old bitch will give us whatever we want to get her back, and we want plenty. Now come over here and let's plan what we're going to do with all that money."

Jerry hadn't wanted to get back into bed. He just wanted a ciga-rette and a cup of coffee with a double shot of bourbon.

Why can't I just tell Kenny that? What the hell is wrong with me? Jerry wondered. But he didn't tell Kenny. Instead, he did what he always did—whatever Kenny (or anyone else) wanted him to do.

He got back into bed. Jerry didn't sleep though. He lay there and wondered, *Why could I stand up to Kenny about sharing Libby but can't stand up to him when it comes to my own needs. What do I really want and need?*

They didn't get back up until noon. Kenny was on fire, ready to "get them all." Jerry just wanted to pull a pillow over his head and go back to sleep.

CHAPTER 6

L ibby was nervous. So was Norma. They sat quietly in the
police station. Neither could believe that months had passed
without any contact from Kenny and Jerry. Their divorces
were granted without any protest because neither Kenny nor Jerry
had shown up in court.

They hadn't asked for anything, except their freedom. Both
Libby and Norma had received restraining orders against them. They
had not fought them as that meant both Jerry and Kenny had to stay
away from them as well. It was a blessing in disguise, they both realized. Life without Kenny or Jerry.

They had both breathed signs of relief to know that they
wouldn't have to have any contact with their former husbands.

"The Lord works in mysterious ways," Norma had commented
to Libby during her phone call, letting Libby know how glad she was
to get her summons to court.

Libby had protested at first. She hadn't wanted it on her record,
but in the end she was thankful as well.

Cody was almost a year old. Libby and her grandmother were
planning a party for Cody at the day care that day, the day Libby

received her summons. They were all living together now. It had been a good year in terms of adjustment.

Grandmother had not only taken them into her home, but into her heart and arms as well. She had actually cried when she saw Cody for the first time.

"How could I have not wanted to reconnect with you?" she had exclaimed when she saw Libby. "And to you, my dear daughter." She hugged Norma. She had sobbed when she saw Cody. "And who are you, little precious one?"

It was hard for Constance to watch her daughter go to work. She had reminded them again this morning as the three of them sat in the front parlor sipping on hot chamomile mint tea. They gathered the mint leaves from Nana's special garden every week so they would be fresh for their weekly teatime together.

"It was such a shock that each of you wanted a career for yourselves. I have enough money to keep us in luxury until way past Cody's lifetime. You wanting to work for Dr. Leonard," she had admitted to Norma, "and you insisting on going to college, young lady, all in the same month! I thought I'd have a stroke. Women in my family just don't hold down jobs." Grandmother loved quoting from her favorite movie, *Gone with the Wind*.

It had been a special moment between all of them. A confirmation that they were headed in the right direction.

"I wish your father could see me now," Grandmother had said to Norma tearfully as her wrinkled hand touched Norma's. "He would be proud of me. He always saw beneath my rough exterior. He was the gentle soul, the one who had the confidence and strength of a mighty king, yet the humility of the lowest servant. It was ironic, because he had very little a few years before I met him, just his little bed and breakfast. I was the one who drove us both crazy with my need to have more, look better than anyone else in town. And he didn't object because money just wasn't important to him the way it was to me."

"Grandmother, I had no idea," Libby whispered. "Mama? How could you have not told me all of this?"

"Because I wouldn't let her talk about him, Libby," Grandmother had said. "I wouldn't let anyone talk about him. But I should have. When he died, my world fell apart. He and I were best friends, truly soul mates. I am breaking my own code of silence though, and it is so cleansing. You will be hearing a lot more about your sweet old grandfather, Libby! God broke the mold when he made Hugo. As I was saying, Libby, whenever I fretted about this or that, he would just smile in his gentle way and say, 'Connie, you worry about the darnedest things. When we get to heaven, it's not going to matter one bit what kind of car we drove, what kind of house we lived in, what kind of clothes you wear. God's going to look at our hearts. He's not going to care one bit about our material belongings.' Then he would take my hands in his and say, 'You know I love you, don't you?' I would smile and kiss him on the cheek. Then he would go about his business, which had been running the registration desk at the small bed and breakfast he owned and where he continued to work for years after we married."

Constance Marie Galyon had been born Constance Marie Henderson. Her mother, Helena Marie Henderson Whittington, had been the owner of a large chain of hotels and restaurants, stretching from Gatlinburg, Tennessee, to Asheville, North Carolina. Helena had been a widow when Connie met Hugo.

"Although my nana was as kind as the day was long, she also was driven by the love of money. She believed if you had money, you had the power to move mountains. Yet she was thrilled that I had married your grandfather, Libby, even though to her he was a pauper. Owning his own bed and breakfast didn't count for much with her.

But she loved his gentle ways and the fact that he was so in love with me! Even though we married on the sly, she had already given us her blessing. What she didn't count on, though, was the ridiculing that had begun even before we married. Even though my friends knew he had more than a decent living, they made fun of his country boy ways."

"You are thinking of marrying him," they had teased her in their judgmental tones.

"I wanted their approval, at least with Hugo." She reached over and touched Norma's hand as a tear slipped down her cheek. "I'm so sorry, dear, so sorry."

Norma hugged her and asked her to continue her story.

"I was already swept off my feet and was determined to marry, stealing away in the night much like you and Jerry did," she said to Libby. "We just couldn't wait to be with each other, you know, in the sexual way. People didn't have sex before marriage in my day."

Libby had been startled that her grandmother was sharing that bit of information. "Mom, you never told me," she said to Norma.

"Honey, I made it so hard on your mother. She was afraid to tell anybody anything." Grandmother again patted Norma's hand lovingly. "I had my reputation to consider, you know."

Norma was glad her mother was finally telling Libby this story about her grandfather. Norma wanted her daughter to see the goodness in her mother, the goodness that had been there before Norma's father had died from that awful Alzheimer disease. After her mother had come back from the funeral, she had been a changed woman, unable to speak for weeks. When she did speak, she sounded just like Grandmother Anne, Hugo's mother, who Norma had feared.

Grandfather had died when Libby was just a child, so she hadn't known him very well. It had been hard on her mother though, who loved him dearly, as did Grandmother who was devastated when he died. Libby was in awe of this part of her grandmother. It was such a sweet part of her to witness, and Libby was grateful for the opportunity.

Grandmother hadn't cared that Hugo hadn't the kind of money her family had. He did own his bed and breakfast, but to the people who lived in Constance Galyon's world, that was nothing. She hadn't cared that he had no status in her world. He was rich in so many ways. Ways that Connie knew, yet very few others knew. She loved him very much, which was, again, surprising to Libby.

Hugo Galyon's father was a coal miner's son, deep in the back woods of Kentucky. A poor country boy, he had worked hard, daily breathing in the coal dust that destroyed his lungs and finally took his life.

He had gotten really sick in his thirties. He had been working in the coal mines since he was sixteen, a dropout from the primary school he attended until the fifth grade.

"He was smarter than any PhD I'd ever met," Grandmother had said when Libby asked her to tell them more about him. "He got a settlement from the Black Lung benefits program, a government program that helped people to live out the remainder of their days easier than they had lived up to that point."

But Grandmother would have given up all their money, she had told them, if in doing that, she could have saved him.

It wasn't to be. Because he had risked almost his entire life on more than one occasion to bring the much-coveted coal to Kentucky homes, he had received a larger settlement than most of his coworkers who had also become sick. Hugo's father had taken most of his check and invested it in the bed and breakfast, which was passed to Hugo at his death.

"Wasn't he scared to invest all of his money?" Norma had asked.

"No, he wasn't." Grandmother had smiled.

"I will just be back where I started," he had said. "Other than this lung problem, I've been a happy man. We've never needed much, until you." He had kissed Grandmother's hand like she was a queen. "God brought you to my son, to us, in His perfect timing."

"Norma, he trusted God with his life. And so did Hugo. He had taken over the bed and breakfast only three months before he came in and swept me right off my feet."

A tear slid down Grandmother's face. Libby wanted to hug her, but she also wanted her to finish the story, so she just held her hands in hers.

He had met Grandmother at a restaurant she and her parents owned. It was an upscale restaurant and hotel. Hugo had just gone in to see about a room for the night. He had been traveling, he had said. "I just need to put my head on a clean pillow and I'll bet your pillows are very clean indeed."

Grandmother remembered their first meeting as if it were yesterday.

"We have more than a clean pillow, sir. We are one of the best hotels along the Blue Ridge Parkway!" Grandmother had replied haughtily.

Hugo later told her he had been fascinated with her feisty nature.

"What can I do to convince you to have breakfast with me in the morning?" he had asked.

Grandmother had said, "Pay your bill and we'll go from there." He had laughed and gone up to his room.

In the morning, Grandmother couldn't keep her eyes off him. She had taken his business card and had looked at it carefully the night before. "Hugo Galyon," she had read the card out loud. She recognized the name of the small bed and breakfast. She wondered whether he washed dishes there or owned the place. He dressed like a country boy. He drove an old car and didn't wave his money around for all to see. It wasn't who he was, he had told her the next morning.

"He was just dreamy," Grandmother said.

Libby just laughed. She had never heard her grandmother talk like that before. It was fun watching her.

Grandmother continued. She wasn't used to being around someone who really didn't care what others thought about him. She and all her friends were very attached to other people's opinions. "Grandmother Anne, especially." Grandmother's stern face appeared then. "She was very harsh, very stern, was a gentle spirit and a very loving mother. I am so happy you gave Cody our middle name." She squeezed Libby's hands. "She was much like your grandfather, always telling me to stop worrying about what other people thought. But it had been too late, as Grandmother Anne had made an indelible mark upon my soul. When my own mother died of a heart attack, and then my father died shortly after, we moved in with Grandmother Anne at her insistence. I was devastated and didn't think about how living with her would affect me emotionally. I missed my mother terribly. I was do depressed. I had even thought about suicide. But in the end, I knew that wasn't the right path. The path I took wasn't either, but I didn't know it until I was already a slave to it, to her, and to all my socialite acquaintances. They made all the decisions, not me." She looked at Norma and smiled. "Oh my God, I became just like them with you, my dear."

She went on, "Grandmother Anne put me in the finest schools, finest clothes, and gave me all the important things in life. At least that's what I was led to believe. She did take care of me when I was so depressed I couldn't take care of myself. For that, I found the grace to forgive her sternness right before she died. She was, after all, Hugo's mother. So she was family. But the damage was done. I turned out just like her, didn't I, Norma?"

Norma looked at her mother and laughed. "Yes, you did," she said. It needed to be said. "Yet I found that same grace to forgive you, Mama." It was the first time Norma had ever felt good calling her mama.

Usually, Grandmother had insisted on *Mother*, a term that Norma found harsh, just like her mother had been most of her life. But as she looked at her now, she saw a very different woman. And if it hadn't been for sweet little Cody, would they ever have found the strength to heal and reconnect? Norma doubted it but wouldn't dismiss the possibility because she now knew that she, alone, was responsible for her own choices, no matter the influences along life's way.

"And now sweet Maria, who had been a part of our family. Her death has been tragic. And the loss of her is harder than I could have imagined." Constance was quite tearful now, so she drank the rest of her tea in silence.

Norma remembered how Maria had cried when her father had died.

"He was like my own poppy," she had sobbed. "We will miss him so much."

That was why she had been at the house the day she was murdered. It was normally her day off, but she had dropped by to check on the renovations since Constance was gone.

Right before Norma, Libby, and Cody had moved in, Grandmother had sold her large restaurant and hotel chain. She had kept the small bed and breakfast that was Hugo's. She didn't work there anymore, but the inn was still doing very well and sometimes she would just go over and help at the reception desk as she had so many times when she had first married Hugo.

"It keeps me grounded," she said whenever anyone would ask why she was working there. Mostly now she was content to focus on her girls, as she liked to call her daughter, granddaughter, and great-granddaughter. "My girls keep me busy," she would say to her poker friends. It was obvious she enjoyed the "work."

A lot had happened since Cody's birth. Norma had agreed to work for Dr. Leonard as his receptionist. He had decided to try private practice again, and it was going well. He and Norma made a great team at the office and at home.

And George and Libby had grown closer and closer during these past few months. He had visited Libby's room the day of her and Cody's discharge. He had gone to take them home. They had to wait, though, because he had been assaulted by Libby's husband, Jerry. He had filed a complaint with the police and then took Libby and Cody home.

George and Libby began seeing each other socially. And, when he felt the time was right, he was going to ask her to marry him. They were very much in love and had already talked about marriage.

"Just too much happening in our worlds right now, my dear. We need to start fresh." He knew that Libby had been through a lot, and so he had told her, "I'm not going to pressure you. But one day soon, I am going to ask you to marry me. I want you to think about that. I love you very much."

Libby had smiled and told him that she also loved him. "I think I chose to love you the first time you stood up for me at that grocery store." She laughed again, telling her mother the story.

Libby had been in line and had just told George her head was hurting and she just wanted to get the groceries and go home. About that time, a man had pushed ahead of her in the line.

George had been looking at a magazine, but he had seen it. He had gone up to the man and told him he had pushed past his wife and it had been unacceptable.

The man had been gruff. "Do you want to take this outside?" he had asked.

George had shaken his head and said, "No need. I have the police on my speed dial. Shall I call them?"

The man had cursed, thrown his groceries down in front of Libby's, and stomped out of the store. The other people in line had clapped in unison.

Libby told George she had never had anyone offer her that kind of support before. "Not ever," she had repeated in the car on the way home.

She and George had gone to the store to get some things Helen had forgotten. Libby wanted to make Cody's birthday cake herself. She was determined to become a good cook, just like her grandfather Hugo had been.

Norma had begun seeing Tom, the priest who had been the hit-and-run survivor that George had operated on. Tom had left the priesthood when Norma had married Kenny. He had moved away. Norma thought he had just transferred to another parish, which was bad enough. She had missed him terribly.

But as Tom had put it, "I couldn't stand knowing you were married to Kenny and I was married to the church. It just didn't seem right. I've made my peace with God. He never intended that a man or a woman should be married to the church. That was all man's idea." He had researched it carefully and had asked for dispensation so that he could begin again.

But he couldn't put Norma out of his mind. "I'll just go and see her one more time," he told himself.

He hadn't wanted to cause any problems for Norma. He just wanted to see her, actually talk to her one last time before he moved on with his life. That's why he was in town. People had just assumed he was still a priest because it was a small town and they recognized him as their former priest. He hadn't even bothered to correct them when several former parish members had stopped to say hello in the diner. Tom was surprised that he still felt so at home there.

Tom had wanted to walk for a while after his meal and clear his head. He hadn't seen Norma since that night at the rectory when she had told him about marrying Kenny. She had been crying. He had held her; and for one night, just one night, they had made love. "The way normal people did when they were in love," he had told himself so many times after she left. He had cried too.

At that time he was still struggling with the church's mandate that he remain single "and leave all his money to the church," he had whispered under his breath, lest anyone know the truth about his research and why the Western church forbade marriage yet the Eastern Rite had to allow it.

If he ever saw Norma again, it was going to be as a different man. He had gone back to school and gotten a doctorate degree in urban and regional planning with an emphasis on tourism and development and preservation of environmentally sensitive areas. He was planning to move to Cancun, Mexico, after he saw Norma. He had already been accepted there to help with protecting their beaches, which were quickly eroding away. He didn't see the car coming!

Cody's birthday was two weeks away. They had all hated to end their very special teatime. It had become a ritual, a cherished time together, to watch each other grow and heal. But Norma and Libby both had errands to run, and Gamma had gone back to bed. Grandmother had been so touched when Cody said, "Gamma."

"You heard the child. That is my name from now on."

On their way to the grocery store Libby had told George about their wonderful time together. She had gone into detail about her grandfather and how she wanted to learn to cook, just as he had.

She had laughed when she described the way Cody had renamed Grandmother. At this particular teatime, Cody had climbed up into Grandmother's lap and said, "Gamma." They had all rejoiced. She truly was a "Gamma" now they had all decided, pleased that Cody had been the first to realize it.

Gamma had rocked little Cody to sleep, and Norma and Libby had gone their separate ways to shop for the big birthday party. They had been hailed by the local sheriff as they were driving out of the driveway to get one more thing Libby had forgotten, the candle for the cake.

They were persons of interest, he had said. Norma and Libby were being detained by the police, pending further investigation into Maria's murder. She had been killed by a Colt 45. Norma's father had owned a Colt 45, and it had disappeared from the house the day Maria was shot.

It was difficult, following the sheriff into town. Both Tom and George wanted to accompany them, but they wanted to do whatever it took to help them find Maria's real killer and wanted to do this alone. Gamma had already told them that she thought Kenny and Jerry had killed her.

They had all kept their promise to each other. They talked openly and freely about their feelings now and about anything that any one of them felt was important to discuss so that they would all be on the same page.

Norma had told Libby as they had headed out to the driveway today, "I feel like you and I and Gamma have just had a CODA meeting. I love our teatimes, and I love what God is doing in all our lives."

Helen had called their progress LUG, in that they were learning, understanding, and growing. The LUG acronym helped them to remember what they were doing. They were learning how to resolve conflicts many have between Christian martyrdom and codependency.

Helen had said, "When we are taking up our cross, the way Jesus suggested we do, it is not an easy task. But as we LUG that cross around, we are in the process of transformation."

Libby told her mom, "I have to admit that I was glad, even in the beginning, that you wanted to spend so much time with Cody. But at the same time, I was a little jealous. Cody adores you, and sometimes I feel left out. But now that I am 'lugging,' as Helen explained, I step behind that initial feeling of jealousy and focus on how very thankful I am that Cody had such a wonderful nana and

Gamma. I hope you don't think I'm awful, but I just had to admit that. I've wanted to for a while, but this seemed the time."

They had reveled in how much they were learning about life and had been laughing and joking about Grandfather Hugo's country ways when the sheriff had stopped their cars. Sheriff Riley had been around for a decade or longer.

Both Norma and Libby had asked why they were stopped. Sheriff Riley asked them to come back to the station with them for questioning related to Maria's death.

"Of course," they both had agreed willingly.

They explained to Riley that they had chosen to forgive Kenny and Jerry but were "ready to fight them to the death if either of them tried to see Cody." They hadn't tried. Yet Maria was dead, and according to Grandmother, Kenny and Jerry had been in the house just before she walked in and found her and she believed they had taken the gun belonging to her husband.

"Shot in cold blood," the policeman was saying. No charges were being made at this time. They just needed statements from them both and they were to remain in town in case they were needed further.

Libby and Norma were relieved but ready to get out of there, so when they saw George, they were ecstatic.

George got to the police station as soon as he could. He had gone on and run some errands of his own while the girls were being questioned. He told the police officer he wasn't surprised that Kenny and Jerry were still causing this family so much grief. "Those two are bad news," he had spoken frankly.

"You don't say?" Officer Riley looked at Norma and Libby. "You just told me you had made your peace with them."

Both women, determined to be completely honest, started telling the officer they had made their peace with the past and had chosen to forgive their abusive behaviors but what George was saying was true.

"They could have done it, but why? Were they looking for Cody?"

Officer Riley was a kind man and believed their stories. He could see the anguish in their faces when they talked about how they feared for their safety and for Cody's safety until Kenny and Jerry were apprehended. They had told the sheriff how they had decided not to fight the restraining orders because they realized they were blessings in disguise. "They have to stay away from us as well!"

Riley saw the women were genuine, and he thought they were being completely honest. But much as he wanted to believe them, Riley had a job to do so he had to continue the questioning.

"So when is the last time you saw them?"

When they told him it had been almost a year, the officer pressed on.

"How can you explain your father's gun missing?" he asked Norma. "If ballistics says it's the murder weapon, you two may be looking at a murder charge. Is there anything else you'd like to add before I let you go?"

Both Norma and Libby had remained silent, other than telling him what Grandmother had told them about seeing Kenny and Jerry.

George had asked the officer if he could take them home since they weren't being charged.

Officer Riley told him to "keep them close in case we need to question them any further."

George agreed, and they all walked slowly to the car.

It was a quiet drive on the way home. They were all in shock that Libby and Norma were even being questioned as possible suspects. They didn't know how much the police knew, and they needed to talk with Grandmother again before anything else was said or done. Grandmother had been fighting the flu for the past four days and had taken Maria's death very hard. She had gotten up for their tea that morning as "wild horses couldn't keep me away from our special time together." But she had gone back to bed.

Maria was such a sweet person. She had been with Connie almost thirty years. She still expected to see her every time she walked into the kitchen. It was Maria's favorite place to be as she saw herself as a top chef and had recently told them, "It is a good thing you have me to cook for you, because how in the world would you feed yourselves?"

It had been true. Gamma had to depend upon Maria as she had rarely cooked for herself or her family.

"Wealthy women don't do that sort of thing," her own husband's grandmother had told her when she married Hugo.

But what Grandmother Anne never knew was how much fun she and her husband had in the kitchen when Hugo decided he needed to whip up some chicken and dumplings. It had been his own mother's recipe, and Gamma had loved them. She had cherished that time the two of them had together.

"Just being ordinary folks," Hugo had told her as he danced with her around the kitchen. "In the end, we are all just ordinary folks, Connie."

Norma spoke first as they walked into the bedroom.

"Mother, the police think that Libby and I are somehow involved in Maria's murder. Officer Riley told us she had been killed with a Colt 45, and they think we might have done it."

"Good heavens, child." Grandmother smiled. "Officer Riley is not keeping up with this case very well."

"What do you mean, Grandmother?" Libby questioned.

Constance looked at her sternly and said, "What is my name?"

Libby had laughed and said, "I mean, Gamma."

"Well, while you were being questioned by Officer Riley, I was on the morning news and I gave a full description of Maria's condition when I found her and I pointed my finger at the likely murderers. Just like I told you this morning, those two got your father's gun and they had to kill Maria to get it. I am sure of it. And now the whole county knows it."

"Gamma, you did that for us?" Libby hugged her tightly, tears falling on her grandmother's hands.

"I have a lot to make amends for child. Yes, I've been reading that Al-Anon book of yours, Norma. You, Libby, and Cody are the most important people in my life. And to tell you the truth, I felt my dear Hugo's spirit right beside me as I let the whole county know that even the Galyon family has skeletons in their closet. It felt good to be honest, to not give a damn what my poker club might think. Now get yourselves together," she said. "I'm going back to bed. I have to be well in two weeks. The two of you had better get busy. We have a birthday party to plan."

Libby smiled and said, "I love you, Gamma."

Her grandmother hugged her tightly and kissed her on the cheek. "I love you too, Libby. I always did. I just let the wrong things become priorities. Thank God I have been given a second chance."

Libby said good-bye to George, and she and her mother sat down to go through all they had bought. Libby finished telling Norma about how George had stepped in front of her at the grocery store and confronted the bully. Norma had smiled, knowing that George was crazy mad about Libby.

"Okay," Norma said. "We have twelve children in Cody's day care, two nannies, Tom, me, George, Gamma, and you, Libby." They were counting the possible attendees. "Is that all?"

"Maria's two sisters would love an invite," Libby offered.

One of them, Serena, was in the school of social work with Libby; and they had become good friends.

"It will be a little crowded, but I think it would do them good to be around something positive at a time like this. And Cody would love seeing Carlos again. Those two have grown so close."

Norma thought it was a wonderful idea and praised Libby for her generosity and thoughtfulness.

"Of course, it would," she said. "Why don't you give them a call right now?"

Libby thanked her for the compliment and left the room thinking she should get a bigger cake.

"I can't wait." She smiled to herself. "And I'll need to charge the battery on my camera. Serena had already promised to help with the party by bringing a piñata for the children to knock down. So many things to do." She hummed as she dialed the number.

Maria's sisters were very grateful to be invited and accepted the offer immediately.

"Shall I bake a cake for her?" Maria's sister had asked.

It gave Libby great joy to tell her, "No, I am baking the cake. Just come on over to the day care and help us celebrate. And bring Carlos with you. We love you all so much."

Meanwhile, in Gamma's room, Cody had crawled over to her nana.

"Come here, my sweet angel." Norma beamed with delight. "You are loved so much, you precious child. Gamma loves you. Nana loves you. Mommy loves you. George loves you. Tom loves you. Is that too many people to love you?"

Norma liked playing this game with Cody. Cody would always clap her hands and say, "Buddy loves Cody." Her vocabulary was growing by leaps and bounds. Just then Cody pulled up to Gamma's bedside table and giggled.

"She'll be walking running before you know it," Gamma exclaimed as she reached down and scooped her up on the bed beside her.

Connie never tired of her time with Cody. And she was positive that Cody would be running by her birthday.

Sure enough, the morning before her first birthday, Cody took off and never looked back.

"She's more than a toddler now," Norma cried. "You know she's going to be into everything."

They had all laughed together. "We will celebrate Cody's birthday and her first steps!"

"Before you know it, she'll be off to school, then off with friends, then off to college, then off to marriage, then probably off to a career somewhere. They grow up so fast." Gamma was tearful. She didn't want to let go of the joy she had experienced these last few months.

Norma came over to where she was sitting and hugged her. Libby walked back into the room about then, and they told her about Cody's first steps. Libby was ecstatic.

She said, "We're here, Grandmother, all of us. And we'll always be a family…always, whether we live here with you or not."

She was already thinking about her and George and Norma and Tom and how they would eventually want a home of their own.

Maybe Gamma will come live with one of us, she thought. *Maybe not now, but when she is no longer able to care for herself. We will care for her, just as she cared for Grandfather Hugo.*

Libby had come to love her grandmother very much. She doubted she would have ever felt this close to her, except for her daughter, Cody. Gamma had slowly gone from a stern and judgmental woman to a more flexible, happy, and very accepting woman, mother, grandmother, and great-grandmother. Libby couldn't be happier with their relationship or the relationship she had with Norma.

Libby went to the kitchen to make them dinner. She missed Maria, waving her spoons and spatulas at her, telling her to "leave my creative atmosphere so I can be alone with my recipes."

She was smiling at that thought when Norma came in to help. She pulled Libby aside.

"I didn't want to say anything to you before now, Libby, but I think I'm being followed. And I don't think it's the first time."

"Mama, you can't be serious. Why would anyone want to follow you?"

Norma explained that she had run into Rick Browning, the CEO from Windows to Your Dreams, less than a week ago and again that morning.

"He's here in North Carolina, Libby. I haven't seen that man in years, not since he fired your father and Jerry and we left Orlando. Now twice in one week. I don't think it's a coincidence. Something's not right, Libby. Maybe Kenny is blackmailing him again. He talked about it. Kenny told me once that Jerry kept a copy of the real accounting books as well as the cooked books, he called them, and that one day they would come in handy." Norma was white-faced. "I always thought it was strange that Rick never went after Kenny after he blackmailed him that one time. But Kenny came away with a more than generous retirement package, so something must have happened between them. Of course, it could be about the photos I found of Rick and Jerry."

She had told Libby all about them.

"Kenny had said that was for insurance when he saw me looking at the photos. He had taken them out of my hands and stuffed them in his briefcase. Neither of us bought it up again. I felt awful for you, Libby, when I saw those photos. But since we had lost touch, I really hadn't thought about any of it, until Maria's death. But, Libby, Rick was quite anxious the last time we talked. Something's up."

"But why would Rick be following you, Mama? Why not Daddy or Jerry?"

Norma responded, "Because your dad and Jerry are hiding out. I'm sure of it. And I am sure that by now, they have seen Mama's interview on the morning news. This is also bizarre, Libby. Maybe Rick is following me in hopes of my leading him to Kenny. Little does he know that we will probably never see either of them again. At least I hope not."

The phone rang, and Norma answered it. It was Tom. He told her he wanted to get Cody a really special gift and needed some help choosing one. Norma told him to pick her up in an hour and she would go shopping with him.

"Try not to worry, Libby," her mother said. "We just have to be careful, that's all."

Norma took a shower and waited for Tom. She had loved him as far back as she could remember, since she was a teenager. He had been the priest of her parish, and he was the youngest and dreamiest priest she had ever met. She had never told him though, until the night before her marriage to Kenny. They had been strictly friends. She hadn't wanted to come between him and the church.

She had let her mind wander back to that night. She had gone to the church to pray, trying to find the courage to marry Kenny. Tom had been there. They hadn't meant to kiss. But when Tom saw her crying, he had held her in her arms and Norma couldn't hide her feeling for him any longer.

She had told him that she loved him and would always love him. Then she had abruptly gotten up to leave. Tom had pulled her back to the pew. They had kissed, gently at first. Then Tom had gotten up to lock the church doors. He came back and led Norma to the rectory. The housekeeper was gone for the weekend. He just couldn't let her leave. He knew what he was about to do and felt no shame in doing it. He loved her. He wanted to be with her.

As he lay her down on his bed, he tenderly explored her body, not like Kenny, who was only interested in pleasing himself. He gently kissed her all over. Norma began undressing him. She pressed her face into his chest and touched the dimples in his cheeks. She loved everything about Tom. She always had. They took their time. It was the sweetest lovemaking Norma had ever experienced.

She stepped out of the shower and dried herself off. Her mind went back to Tom. She remembered the first time. They had taken things slowly. Then came the waves of pleasure. She had gasped. It was the first time for her. Norma had never felt such pleasure. Then Tom had whispered into her hair, "I love you, Norma Galyon. I want to ask for dispensation and marry you. The night I entered the priesthood I had such mixed feelings. I felt I had to choose between allowing myself to love a woman and my love for God, which at that time, I couldn't separate from the Catholic Church. It was so wrong. I was so confused. I hadn't been able to stop thinking about you and then hearing you were marrying Kenny. It was too much. Remember how we used to talk about the corruptions I had witnessed. Remember the anger I felt about the child molestations that were being swept under the rug? Remember the baby I wasn't allowed to Christen in the church because her mother wasn't married? The church is not my God. They help us to feel close to God, but that's all. God is within us. My loving you hasn't taken away my love for God. It has made it stronger. Marry me, Norma, please."

Norma had wanted to say yes. She had even nodded and smiled.

"You were never one to take orders, Tom. If I remember correctly you baptized that baby at a family party the next week, the one the senior priest refused to baptize because her mother wasn't married? I so admired you for it. That Spanish family. I so admired you for it. But this is different, Tom." She had gotten up, shaken her head, grabbed her clothes, and ran out crying. "No, I can't come between you and the church. I would regret it for the rest of our lives. We both would."

She had cried all the way home. She would never forget what her mother had said to her, "I know where you've been, Norma." Norma had admitted to her mother exactly where she had been and what she had been doing. She had hoped that her mother would tell her to run back to the church and say yes to Tom, to accept his proposal. But that didn't happen.

Her mother had been very angry and told her to get a good night's sleep because she would put this behind her and she would marry Kenny the next morning Norma had cried herself to sleep that night and so many nights after. Kenny hadn't seemed to notice, and her mother hadn't seemed to care, or if she did, she never showed it. Norma's mother at that time rarely showed her emotions.

Tom had left town the next day, and Norma had married Kenny. She had brought two wealthy families together. Norma cried a lot at first, but she was determined to "do what Mother thinks is right."

She grimaced now as she got herself dressed. Looking back, she realized that she had made Tom's decision for him. She hadn't given him a chance to decide for himself. "God, how in the world do we really know what is right?"

CHAPTER 7

When Rick Browning had become CEO, Window to Your Dreams had made more money than it had ever made. He was able to convince the board to buy up some smaller vacation clubs, and they had quickly become a conglomerate. No other time-share company could equal their sales or their products.

He wasn't sorry he had let Kenny and Jerry go. He didn't need that kind of publicity. And he didn't really like either of them, he often quipped to his wife.

Little did she know the real reason Rick had to get them out of his sight! They sickened him, and not just because they were gay! They held something over his head that no one should have to live with. And as the years went on, it wasn't enough they were gone from his business. He wanted them dead!

It hadn't been hard for Rick to find another CPA who was just as willing to be corrupt as Jerry had been. They weren't hurting in the sales department either.

"Money talks," Rick had said more than once.

Rick just couldn't get Kenny out of his mind though. Yes, Kenny had stopped the blackmail when he moved away. But had he kept a copy of that video? Rick just couldn't move past "the nerve of that guy even trying to blackmail me at all." His fists clenched, and his face got red with anger just thinking about Kenny. And lately, he was all he thought about.

Does he still have those photos and that video of me and Jerry? Does Jerry still have evidenced that we cheated our customers?

He couldn't get these questions out of his mind. It was driving him crazy trying to figure out if his reputation was safe or not, not to mention the negative publicity for his company. His fears had become an obsession, to the point that Rick retired early and moved to North Carolina where his family of origin was from. The mountain home had been empty for years, and his wife was more than excited about the renovations.

Window to Your Dreams had been Rick's baby. He had built the company up into a conglomerate, and he was proud of his accomplishments. The money he made bought him anything he wanted, including a beautiful wife, twenty years his junior, and the best prostitutes available!

Kenny and Jerry hadn't tried to contact Rick since he had fired them. He wished he could just move on, but his pride wouldn't let him.

"Nobody screws Rick Browning and gets away with it," he told himself almost daily now.

He was willing to risk everything to get revenge. He even toyed with the idea of killing Kenny and Jerry and had even begun thinking about how he would do it.

He couldn't believe his luck when he found out that Kenny and Jerry had also moved to western Carolina!

Almost like fate. He grinned to himself when he had run into Kenny's wife that very first year!

He had started following her. That had been a bust so far. But when Norma noticed him standing right outside her office, she had walked right up to him and said hello. That's when his luck changed. She told him that she and Kenny were divorced. She had a baby with her. She had to be Kenny's grandchild. That's when he began to formulate his plan. He could kidnap the child and use her as ransom to get to Kenny. He thought about it for weeks. Then it happened!

Rick had just seen Norma's mother on the news that morning. She was strikingly beautiful, even at her age! Rick was envious of her and her husband, Hugo, always wondering who had the most money. It wasn't about the money though. He didn't like the idea of kidnapping her great-granddaughter. He really liked children and had respect for Hugo, but it was the only way to get to Kenny and humiliate him the way he and Jerry had humiliated him!

Once he had him, he would get rid of him and set up his lover, Jerry, to take the fall. That would get them both out of the way. Yes, Rick knew that Kenny and Jerry were lovers. Everyone at the office did even though they tried hard to hide it. Rick really hadn't cared, but his wife badgered him to death about it.

"Do you really want those kinds of people working for you?" she had asked him more than once.

What she didn't know was that Kenny had made it look like he was one of them. The photos were bad enough, and Rick didn't even allow himself to think about the video. It was disgusting! He wouldn't admit it to a living soul, but he often wondered if he had enjoyed it. Jerry had slipped something into his drink that had pretty much knocked Rick out. He remembered little. Rick had never engaged in homosexual activities before but had wondered about how Kenny and Jerry could be that way. He tensed up when he remembered the night after their final office party together.

He had gotten drunk; and the alcohol, with whatever they had slipped into his drink, rendered Rick helpless, totally helpless. Jerry had taken advantage of him, sexually, and he could barely remember anything, just that Jerry and Kenny kept giving him shots of tequila and he kept downing them.

He didn't want to appear as if he couldn't hold his liquor. It was right after he had told them he was letting them go. Kenny had smiled, saying he was "ready to retire anyway." Rick knew he was livid, but Kenny had a way of hiding his real feelings, making everyone around him think he was completely in control.

The drinks kept coming. "Let's get that bottle of tequila out of the refrigerator and celebrate." Kenny had chuckled. God, he hated that man!

He was fuzzy about the details, but he vividly recalled getting in the elevator with Kenny and Jerry. He vividly remembered sitting down on the couch in his penthouse. They had gone together to get the new bottle of tequila Rick had just brought back from Mexico. The rest was a blur.

He flashed back to waking up with his pants around his ankles. Kenny was slapping his face, waving a legal document, a video tape, and photos. The photos showed him and Jerry in a most compromising act of sex.

The document stated that Kenny and Jerry were to get an astronomical severance pay. Rick had planned to give them nothing. He was so angry, he thought he'd have a stroke, but had agreed to everything they wanted. He then signed the document, and Kenny had given him the video and photos.

"Our only copies," Kenny had said with a smile.

Shortly afterwards Rick filed a suit against them for fraud against their customers. Rick thought that would be revenge enough. But it wasn't. The suit was quietly dropped. Jerry said he'd love nothing better than taking the judge out to dinner and showing him his original set of books before Rick had asked him to keep a second set. Rick knew he had been robbed, and they would pay!

Rick didn't want to take any chances with Jerry. He could go from calm to a raving maniac in seconds.

Jerry is probably the one who pulled the trigger on that maid, Rick thought. He always did have that violent temper, at least when he worked at Window to Your Dreams, so he would go after Kenny.

Rick figured if he followed Jerry, he would find Kenny, but he hadn't been able to find either of them. They were probably long gone or hiding very well. The interview with Norma's mother that morning was an astonishing stroke of luck!

When he had "run into" Norma the second time, she had been holding a little girl. She hadn't offered Rick any information about the child, but it had to be Kenny's granddaughter, Jerry's daughter. It had to be. Rick had smacked his lips when he walked back to his car. He had figured out how he would get to Kenny.

"Okay, following Norma wasn't such a bad idea after all," he had muttered to himself.

He would follow her home the next time. But he had to be careful. She would definitely be suspicious if they "accidentally" met again, especially at her work.

A week later Rick had gone back to the medical clinic where he knew Norma worked. He had sat across the street at a newspaper stand. He had looked through the paper for a solid hour before Norma had walked out. But then she was finally walking to her car.

He followed her to her Lexus, then quickly ran to his own. He ran a red light but managed to keep that beautiful Lexus (newer than his) and her in sight. He whistled under his breath when he saw the estate drive she turned into. Winding along a row of mountain laurels, he followed along the perfectly landscaped gardens until she finally pulled up to the circular drive out front of her mother's estate.

He knew Norma's mother was rich but never dreamed she was this rich. The mansion was spectacular. He almost forgot why he was there but quickly gained his composure and pulled into the back of some bushes.

He was out of sight, at least he hoped he was. He was staring at the most beautiful view of the Blue Ridge Mountains he had ever seen. It was almost tranquil. He decided he could sit here all evening if he had to. He was worried enough about the video and photos to wait as long as necessary to come back over and over again if he had to.

Six hours passed. Rick fell asleep. Next thing he knew it was morning, and Jerry's wife was pulling out of the gate. He ducked down but not before he saw a kid in a car seat. She looked like the same kid Norma had been holding the last time they "ran into" each other. He took a couple of photos. Then he waited.

She didn't look a thing like Kenny or even Jerry. But Rick knew she had to be related. Why else would Libby have her in the car? He had grinned to himself. "You, my friend, have hit pay dirt."

When he was sure it was safe, Rick pulled out behind her. He followed her to the day care center, putting the final touches on his plan. He would have the little girl kidnapped. He wouldn't hurt her. After all, she was just a kid. Then Kenny would come out of hiding!

"That bastard will feel the fear I did. The fear I live with on a daily basis."

Thinking about the photos of himself and Jerry made him feel so ashamed. He couldn't even remember what it had felt like, but Kenny had taken some very detailed photos. Rick had destroyed everything he had been given as soon as he had gotten the opportunity to do so. But he knew they were only copies. Did they think he was stupid?

At first Rick had been sure Kenny wanted him to lose Windows to Your Dreams. Even though the amount was way too much for severance, it wouldn't make a dent in the company's overall net worth, considering how valuable the company was. And as much as Rick loved money, it wasn't the money he resented. It was about being forced to do anything. After all, he was Rick Browning, the most powerful man in Orlando, Florida, and now in Cashiers, North Carolina, now that Hugo Galyon was dead. He may have retired, but he had lots of plans.

After Rick was sure Libby had left the day care, he went inside to inquire about their rates and availability. He told them, "I promised by daughter I would check into the toddler classes." Telling them he was a retired dentist, Rick had gotten the information he needed. And he was sure they hadn't a clue as to who he really was.

"I've heard such wonderful things about this place, and I only want the best for my grandson," he had cooed. "A Child's World is the best there is, right?"

Filling out an application with a fake name and address, of course, Rick had happened to notice there was a poster on the wall announcing an upcoming birthday party for one of the children. Some kid named Cody.

He didn't notice the last name, but that party would get him in the door. He decided that would be the time he would take the kid he had seen with Libby and Norma. It would be easier at the party with lots of kids, staff, parents, and grandparents around. He remembered the photos he had taken earlier when she was in the car seat when Libby had pulled out of the front gate, so identifying her shouldn't be difficult. He wished he could walk around the room and look at all the children to be absolutely sure, but they were already across the room lined up to go outside.

"It's okay," he told himself. "I got a good photo earlier."

Now who could he get to bring in a birthday present for this little Cody? That would be tricky. Rick was dishonest and ruthless when it came to selling time-shares, but kidnapping, especially an innocent child? That was out of his comfort zone. And he couldn't exactly look in the yellow pages.

"Okay, old boy, you found a highly talented accountant and have trained many highly talented sales agents. All it takes is the right amount of money to get any type of talent one needs, and you are rolling in it." He chuckled to himself.

Rick was happy with his plan. He would just find somebody who needed money, lots of money. Someone who would do whatever he was asked to do for that money. Kenny and Jerry had. So had all his other deceitful sales agents. They knew why they got that extraordinary bonus at Christmastime.

He drove to a seedy part of the neighboring town and parked outside a diner. He was almost afraid to leave his car outside.

"Do it, man, just do it," he chastised himself for being so nervous.

Rick walked inside to order some coffee and waited. He looked out of place in his expensive business suit.

Maybe they'll think I'm a drug lord or something, he thought. *One that knows how to dress well.*

A waitress came back with his coffee and asked, "You're not from around here, are you, mister?"

Rick explained that he was just passing through on his way to South Carolina. He had "noticed the diner and I was hungry."

Lying was something Rick knew how to do. Hell, he was a master of deception. He had turned Window to Your Dreams into the biggest time-share company in the world, hadn't he?

"Creative advertising," he had called it. Not exactly inaccurate, just not totally accurate. He was smooth as silk as he answered her.

She smiled at him and said, "Well, when you gotta eat. Okay, here's your coffee. I'll be back in a few minutes to see what you want to eat."

Rick ordered the daily special, a hamburger with Swiss cheese and fries on the side. As he was trying to decide whether to actually eat the burger or not, he noticed a couple of seedy-looking guys outside next to his Lexus.

They were exchanging a paper bag and a newspaper.

That's odd, Rick thought. Then he realized the transaction was probably drug related. *A real drug deal going down*. He smiled to himself. *A real honest to goodness drug deal*. Rick had been sheltered all his life, and he found this exciting.

He had only seen drug deals go down on TV. Watching the two men was exhilarating, but it also made him nervous, very nervous. He waited until they stepped off the curb to leave, threw some money on the table, and followed them a few steps down the street.

"I saw you admiring my car. I thought you were going to steal it for a minute there," he offered awkwardly.

"What do you take us for?" One of the guys stepped in front of the other and faced Rick head on. "Well, we just might do that, old man."

Rick was sweating profusely, but he played the game. "Why don't I just buy you a car?"

The two guys looked at each other and back at Rick as if he were crazy.

"Why don't we just take yours?" the younger man said with a sneer.

The older one said, "Now hold on here. This nice gentleman wants to buy us a car. We can at least listen to him, can't we?"

"I want you to kidnap a little girl and bring her to me. I don't want you to hurt her in any way, mind you. Kids are innocents. It's her grandfather I want. But if you bring her to me, I will reward you with a new set of wheels. You don't do anything except bring me the girl. You'll get some cash as well. Her grandfather will come to get her. I'll take care of the grandfather, then let the child go. And then you'll get your car. I'll pay you half your cash now and half when it's over."

"Who's the kid?" the older one asked. He was clearly the authority figure, but the younger man was the one Rick was afraid of as he had a very short fuse.

Rick showed them a photo he had taken of Kenny's grand-daughter in her car seat. "I don't know her name, but that's not important. This is a good photo of her showing her face very well. You shouldn't have any problems. She'll be at the party. Just get her and call me at this number when you've done it." He shoved a piece of paper at the man.

Rick took out a new throwaway cell phone, one he'd just bought at the corner store. It was prepaid, like the ones he'd seen on TV. There would be no way they could trace it back to him as he had worn gloves and left no prints on it. Rick's anxiety was mounting.

They seemed to be thinking about it when the younger man spoke up. "You did mean a car for each of us, right?"

Rick was appalled. He felt just like he did when Kenny had blackmailed him into the severance package for him and Jerry.

"You are out of your mind," he snapped and headed for his car. Now he was really afraid. What if these two came after him and stole his car?

The older guy stepped forward. "Stop," he called out. "Come back here. My friend is a little hotheaded."

Rick walked back, forcing one foot in front of the other. He stopped and asked, "Yes?"

The older guy said, "Hey, man, we're businessmen just like yourself. Of course, we try to do as well as we can, just like I'm sure that you do."

Rick had to smile at that one. "Yes," Rick said. "I can understand that, but I can't buy two cars for you, not like mine anyway. I don't have that kind of money."

"Why don't you just pay each of us $25,000 now and the other $25,000 when we get the kid. We'll buy our own cars."

Rick thought about it and agreed. The amount was staggering. One hundred thousand dollars to get to Kenny? But it was worth it to be free of this fear. It was killing him.

They followed Rick to his car. Rick told them to meet him there tomorrow morning. He would have the money.

They said, "Okay, we will be there."

"Don't be late," Rick called back behind him as he got into his car. He was feeling less afraid and rather proud of himself.

Except for the amount he had been forced to pay, things had gone well. He would pay them the cash tomorrow morning. And maybe he would just accidentally forget to bring the balance when they meet again. Rick was a shark when it came to money. He would have the kid by then, and he would have a gun. What could they do?

Rick decided he would take the money out of the corporate account. Who would know? He would doctor the numbers himself just as he had seen Jerry doing time and time again. He would tell the new CPA, Tim, to look the other way and not ask questions if he became suspicious. Tim wouldn't mind. He was still green, but he knew who was boss. Rick was a powerful man, and no one dared to question his orders.

"Money does talk," he reminded himself. He went to the bank, got the cash, and headed across town to his own home, very tired, yet very pleased with himself. "I'd have been a great gangster." He laughed as he walked through the front garden into his house.

He was thinking about Constance Galyon's estate. It bothered him that he liked it better than his own. The view of the lake couldn't compare to his own.

Now that he was home, he drew his attention back to the job at hand. "It's going to work," he said to himself. He would give them a present for the party. It would work! He would be nice to the kid. He didn't want to scare her after all.

After they had delivered the child to Rick, they would call Constance Galyon and tell her they had kidnapped her granddaughter. They would demand that she bring Kenny to exchange for the kid.

"She'll be surprised they don't want any money." He laughed out loud. "This is the best plan I've ever had. Maybe I'll actually be able to sleep at night once I know Kenny and Jerry are taken care of."

What Rick didn't count on was the fact that those two "losers" he had chosen for the job were smarter than he gave them credit for. Unbeknownst to Rick, they were already discussing the options that had been dropped in their own laps.

"If this kid is worth that much money to this chump, how much is she going to be worth to her parents?" Laughing at their dumb luck, they had decided to further explore option number two.

CHAPTER 8

"Today's the big day!" Libby almost shouted as she knocked on her mother's bedroom door. "Mama, are you awake?"

"I've been awake for a while, Libby. Come on in." Norma had a strange look on her face, kind of like she used to look when she was trying to help Libby work a puzzle. Norma told Libby that she had a bad feeling. "I don't know what it is, Libby, but something's not right."

Libby had learned to trust her mother's instincts about certain things. She knew this was one of those things.

"It should be a joyous occasion," Norma exclaimed. "But I'm trying to trust my gut, and my gut is telling me something bad might happen today. I woke up thinking about it. Do you remember my telling you about seeing Rick Browning? Do you remember what he looks like?"

Libby nodded. "Yes, I always thought he looked very distinguished."

Norma continued, "Libby, I can't shake the feeling that his following me had been for a purpose. I keep asking myself why Rick Browning would be following me? What if he tried to hurt Cody to get back at Kenny?"

Libby squeezed her mother's hand. "Mama, I respect your instincts, but I so hope you are wrong about this one. Why in the world would Mr. Browning hurt Cody? It's Dad he's angry at. I'm sure if he wanted to he would hunt him down and shoot him in cold blood after what he and Jerry did to him."

Norma had told Libby about the compromising photos she had found in Kenny's desk drawer.

"You may be right, dear." Norma tried to smile. "But just in case, we'll watch Cody like a hawk at the birthday party, right?"

"Of course, we will, Mama. And there's going to be lots of us there to do the watching. Now get dressed and try to be happy. We have a joyous occasion to attend."

Norma was grateful Libby had been kind with her words and hadn't ridiculed her for her fears the way Kenny used to do. Norma had always had this kind of sixth sense premonition, sensing whether something bad was about to happen. And whenever she told Kenny about one of her "feelings," he would just laugh. But not Libby. She appreciated her mother's gift, whatever it was.

They were human. And they had their arguments, plenty of them, in fact. Both had fiery tempers and said things in anger that they later wished they hadn't. But forgiveness had always been a high priority for Norma and Libby, and they chose it often. It was amazing how honesty played a role in their overall healing. Libby could scream the most hurtful words in a fit of anger. So could Norma. It was Gamma who taught them that honesty was the best policy in terms of "I meant it when I said it. But I love you above all else and always will!" A policy they had all put into practice and were teaching Cody as well.

They had been through so much it was hard to put the past behind them, especially with Jerry and Kenny still at large. They recently watched a news reporter talking about them both.

"They are considered armed and dangerous."

Libby reminded her mother of what Helen had said at their last conjoint session.

"You both will know when the time is right to let go of your fears regarding your ex-husbands. Fears can be very helpful when there is a valid threat. Kenny and Jerry certainly fall into that category."

Helen had also talked to the about post-traumatic stress and how being a survivor of domestic violence and sexual abuse had placed them at risk for being on "high alert," as Norma called it. Norma did have flashbacks of Kenny hitting her with his fist, as did Libby, recalling the time Jerry had hit her with the ball bat and punched her in the stomach. She also had flashbacks to Kenny's abuse. They were indeed hypervigilant when it came to their safety now and especially to Cody's safety.

Cody toddled into the room along with Gamma, who was using a cane but feeling much better than she had in weeks.

"Get dressed, girls." She laughed. "We have a party to attend."

Cody laughed, clapped her hands, and said, "My birfday."

They all reached to hug her at once. It was a sweet moment.

Cody was a smart little girl. She held on to Gamma's cane and started down the stairs. Libby promised she would be right behind them. She still had to put her shoes on, but most importantly, Libby needed to pray.

They were all so proud of Cody. They had talked about the book by Hillary Clinton entitled *It Takes a Community to Raise a Child.* They had been that community for Cody. They all wanted to mother her, which was great in some respects, but it did cause arguments. Gamma and Nana tried to be careful not to step across the boundaries Libby had set regarding the way she wanted to parent. Of course, they spoiled her often, but Libby had been okay with these indiscretions as it was a grandparent's joy to commit them. Libby was so grateful that Cody had both Nana and Gamma to spoil her.

"Dear God," Libby prayed. "Please help us to enjoy today and help us make it a day of peace and joy." Libby was very careful to remind herself that she had her own responsibility related to whether the day might be one of peace or not.

She remembered a session she had with Helen recently in which a part of her felt like a puppet on a string, related to her fears. But as far as God was concerned, "his will is going to prevail." She was glad she was not in control of the behaviors of others, yet she still found it difficult to assume responsibility for her actions when others were at fault, whether it was a huge indiscretion or a tiny one.

"Good from evil," Libby remembered saying to her mother when she was still in the hospital. "She is the good that we all needed, that's for sure," Libby whispered to God. "Thank you for her life. Thank you that Cody entered our lives at just the right time. Your timing, God, as it certainly wouldn't have been mine. Help me to forgive her father, whoever he is. Help me to wish them both good because I still hate them both so much. Please take the hatred away, God, in Your timing, I pray."

Libby pulled her shoes on and started down the stairs. She could hear Cody giggling below. "Cody Marie is a fitting name for her," she whispered. She sat down on the bottom step and continued praying. She wiped a tear from her cheek. "Dear God, help me to focus on the fact that she is here, that I couldn't go through an abortion. Help me to let go of the feelings about how she came to me and just be grateful that she came to me. Grateful that You brought all of us back together, me and Mama and Gamma. Thank you also that You brought Mama and Tom back together and thank you that You brought George into our lives."

Libby was crying tears of joy as she walked into the kitchen. She knew that she would one day have to tell Cody about how she was conceived and named. She would teach her about codependence, the type of behaviors that women and men sometimes escaped to when they hadn't yet learned how to state their needs, then attempt to get them met appropriately without hurting themselves or someone else. She would model for her self-love as well as love of neighbor.

She would tell her that it is okay to love the seemingly unlovable, as long as she didn't lose herself in the process. She would teach her to find the good in all people. Libby believed that was the most important legacy she could pass down to her daughter. She would also help her to realize that codependency is a temporary part of all of us, not dangerous to visit, just dangerous to stay there.

She would teach her that she considered herself, Gamma, and Norma to be saints, trying to return love for hatred, trying to see the good in people when there was so much evil in the world. Cody would learn a more balanced approach to relationships.

Cody would come to understand that her mother and grandmother and great-grandmother were winning the battle for peace in their lives one day at a time and that their main goal was to bear no hatred toward anyone.

Libby wondered sometimes who Cody's father was, but she just couldn't bring herself to think about it very much. "All in good time, Lord, all in good time." She was so grateful that Cody had taken after her mother's side of the family in her physical appearance. Libby knew she would continue loving Cody no matter who she grew up looking like.

Cody had blond hair and dark-blue eyes, and she was very fair skinned. Constance Marie had been very fair, and when she was young, she wore her blond hair in ringlets. Her dark-blue eyes had mesmerized Hugo.

"The joy of codependence," she would tell Cody, "is knowing that even though a part of you is, at times, codependent, it is okay because you will have other parts that fiercely love you."

Nana was already telling Cody the story of the two wolves and how important it was to feed the kind and patient wolf rather than the angry, bitter one. Helen had told them the story, and they all loved it.

Cody would learn the difference between falling in love and choosing to love. She would be more prepared for the dangers of this world than Gamma, Norma, and Libby had been. Libby was already shaking her head, as if to remind herself that Cody would also have fun, lots of fun! She did not want to shelter her from the dangers as much as she wanted to educate her about them.

They would discuss the risks involved with alcohol and drug addictions. Libby would talk to her about abuse, all the different kinds of abuse. Cody would be well-educated and hopefully make better choices than they had. Of course, in the end, Cody would make her own choices and her own mistakes. That was the ultimate joy of freedom.

"None of us are puppets on a string, Libby," she could hear Helen's voice echo in her mind. "We are free to make our own choices, whether good or bad."

Libby listened to Cody's babbling, laughing at Gamma and Nana as they answered her.

"We are going to be okay," Libby said to herself as she tried to shake her mother's worry about the day.

Libby thought back to a recent session. Helen explained to her that it took courage to look evil in the eye and refuse to run from it. It took courage to say, "I am going to give this relationship all that I have to give. If I start losing myself in the process however, if I become empty, if I can clearly see that my love and my sacrifices are not wanted or appreciated, I will courageously walk away, without shame, without regret."

She had asked Libby to recite her new motto whenever she felt stuck in a bad place. Libby was intelligent enough to know that she was not immune to regressing, but she now had a tremendous hope that had previously alluded her. "I will be able to look myself in the mirror at the day's end and claim victory over evil. I will say to myself, 'I did the best I could with what I had today.'"

Helen had reminded her that she needed to fill her mind with that evening mantra.

Gamma was trying to rush them all out the door. They had all managed to get into the kitchen, but no one wanted to go to the car. Libby laughed out loud as it dawned on her what difficulties they would all have strapping Cody into her car seat. Libby had wanted to walk to her day care.

"Fiercely independent, that one," Gamma had said, as she reminded Libby it was her turn to be the "bad guy."

It was a running joke with them, but each of them took turns being the "bad guy" who enforced certain rules like buckling into the dreaded car seat.

Cody continued to babble about her "birfday." Libby was now trying to keep herself calm. She had already zoned out, thinking about this morning's conversation with her mother.

Drifting back to conscious thought, Libby could hear Cody talking to her Nana.

"Here, Nana." It was amazing how well she could communicate at only one year of age. She was telling Norma where she wanted her pink bow, the one that mysteriously kept falling out of her hair.

"Back to the bathroom we go, sweet angel. Let's see if we can get it in a little tighter this time."

Norma gladly obliged with the bow. She had let Cody pick out her bow and birthday dress this morning. They were all convinced about the importance of letting small children make their own choices whenever possible. Libby had read all about this parenting style and firmly believed in its validity.

When she had read the paragraph out loud during one of their morning teas, Norma had teared up. Gamma had seen it. She had gotten up, walked across the room, and hugged Norma.

"It is never too late, Norma," she had said with tears in her own eyes. It had not gone unnoticed that Gamma had patted the back of Norma's new haircut. "Never too late."

Norma had laid out three dresses that Cody could choose from. Cody chose the purple one, which didn't really go with the pink bow she had also chosen, but it wasn't something to argue with her about. There would be time enough for that when more important issues came up over the years.

While they were in the bathroom, which was Norma's "hair salon," Libby had taken the opportunity to have more ginger tea.

She was glad for the time to sit back, relax, and reflect on her life thus far. Helen had told her it was important to remind herself on occasion how far she had come in her healing. Libby put her feet up and recalled her childhood with mixed emotions.

She could still focus on the good, yet she had learned from Helen not to dismiss the bad. It was all part of who she was—the good, bad, and ugly. Helen had explained that each part of who she was needed to be honored. They had worked hard on this area of recovery, and Libby could now better understand the choices that she had made, from early childhood until today.

She knew now that she had chosen Jerry because she desperately needed support and he had offered it. He, as well as Libby, had lived through hell in their childhoods and both had made it out. Not without scars though.

Libby had been too afraid to tell any of her friends what was going on with her father. She had tried in vain to tell her mother. And telling her grandmother had certainly been out of the question at the time. "The best I could do with what I had," Libby smiled to herself.

Libby smiled again as she thought about Cody's future. Libby was sure that Cody would feel free to come to any one of them and talk about difficult issues. They had all promised each other they would be there for her, open, truthful, yet nonjudgmental. And it had been working most of the time.

They all wanted to be there for Cody as well as keep turning the pages in their own lives. Libby was determined to seek input from her mother and grandmother because they had lived in this world longer than she had. Sometimes she felt a little jealous that Cody adored her Nana so much. At those times, however, she reminded herself how grateful she was that Cody had a nana that adored her in return.

"Wisdom comes with age and experience," she had read in one of the books Helen had loaned her. She loved and trusted the combined wisdom of her mother and grandmother. She was developing her own parenting style however, which Norma and Gamma had embraced, even when they didn't quite agree with it. There had been plenty of those times.

Libby smiled as she remembered both Norma and Gamma being appalled that Cody was allowed to cut her own food with a knife. It was under Libby's guidance, but they had still been quite concerned. They had also given her a hard time when she had put Cody in her bassinet with only one blanket over her.

"A baby needs to be swaddled," Norma had said.

Libby had told her mama, "You can swaddle her all you want when you are putting her to bed."

Gamma had just shaken her head and walked out of the room. She had gone back later and covered Cody up, snugly tucking her blanket around her. Libby had seen her do it. She had just smiled. She was more mature now and knew Gamma wasn't trying to undermine her, as much as she was trying to make sure Cody was warm.

Libby admitted to herself that she didn't have all the answers. In fact, even the most popular parenting styles differed in so many ways. She felt very strongly about letting Cody choose her own path though, which included when she was old enough to tell them whether she needed to be covered.

"We made our mistakes, Libby," she recalled Gamma telling her. "We will try not to get in the way of you making yours."

Libby knew Gamma was referring to the swaddling issue, but Libby had not felt chastised. She could have let that remark cause an argument, but she had matured so much and realized it wasn't worth an argument, so she had just smiled.

Both Norma and Gamma had promised her that "Okay, if we want you to consider another option, we will speak up, but in the end, we will honor your decisions."

Gamma had nodded in agreement when Norma voiced the promise. She murmured under her breath however, "That is, if we can't convince you otherwise."

Libby heard her of course. She just smiled.

They had also agreed they would expose Cody to the challenges of the world. No one would shelter her. Libby had discussed that with Helen, who had agreed wholeheartedly.

"Children are far more resilient when they have been allowed to experience sadness, fear, anger, illnesses, even death with appropriate support. If they don't experience these things, how can they learn to manage their emotions appropriately?"

Libby knew it would be wrong to shelter Cody. She remembered a time when her best friend's dog had died. He had been with the family for over ten years. Her friend's stepmother (who was a child therapist herself) let Carly pet the dog as it was lying there dead in their backyard. Carly's stepmom was explaining to her and Libby that the dog's body was there and it was okay to feel sad about him because she would miss him a lot, but the dog's spirit, the best part of him, was already on its way to God. Libby and Carly had been about four or five years old when the dog had died.

Libby remembered Carly's aunt running over to her stepmother and grabbing Carly out of her arms. "She shouldn't be seeing this," her aunt had yelled and had taken Carly back to the porch with her.

Carly's stepmother remained really cool through it all. She did not get angry about the aunt's ignorance.

She and Carly would have plenty of time to talk about Brady and grieve together. Libby had loved Carly's stepmom. She had been so smart in understanding feelings.

Libby had been there for Carly when her dear stepmother had died. They were almost sixteen at the time. It was one of the hardest things Carly had ever experienced. Her stepmother understood, more than anyone else, how important it was to talk about death and dying as a natural part of life.

Carly's mother and sister were like Libby's grandmother used to be. No one was allowed to express their emotions about death or anything else for that matter.

Libby was determined that she would be more like Pat, Carly's stepmom. She and Norma and Constance would all teach Cody together. They all agreed they had their heads in the sand for years trying to pretend that bad things didn't exist. Better to focus on the good.

"Both must be acknowledged," Helen had explained.

Libby wanted Cody to know that evil does exist while at the same time helping her to courageously face it head on.

They had come so far since that terribly, yet joyful, night that Cody had decided to come into this world. Libby was proud of the fact that she had tried to love Jerry and that she had wanted a better life for him. She also was proud of the fact that she had learned to put it all in a more balanced perspective as Helen had suggested. She still believed Jerry had some good in him. He was just so needy, so hungry for love. Libby knew what that felt like, and it helped her not to hate him so much.

Libby would teach Cody that it was important, in the end, to make choices based on what was best for all, whenever possible, but not to let what was best for others choke out her own needs and values. She would tell her daughter about her own fears, at the age of seventeen, being pregnant and believing at that time that had she told her mother or grandmother that she was pregnant and didn't know who the father was they would have disowned her or forced her to have an abortion.

She would also admit to Cody that she didn't have any real evidence to support her fears. And she would encourage Cody to look for evidence before she made inappropriate decisions based on assumptions only.

Cody would be encouraged to develop a balanced approach to life while gaining insights from experts in the field such as Wayne Dyer, Oprah Winfrey, and Marianne Williamson, Libby's all-time favorite resources for growth and healing.

She believed in their teachings, including the one about all her life experiences being blessings. That truth had originally been a stumbling block for Libby, but Helen had helped her there as well.

"There are many different types of blessings," she had said. She had agreed with Libby that marriage to Jerry, at that particular time in Libby's life, had indeed been a blessing. "You needed support, someone you could talk to about abuses, someone your felt safe confiding in, someone who understood. Jerry was that person. You saw his as the only way you could escape the sexual abuse at home."

They had discussed the merits of the Crisis Theory, which taught that it was out of a crisis that one could potentially experience the strongest growth.

"Dr. Leonard coming along when he did, that was a blessing as well. Some blessings bring us to a deeper level of understanding. Others provide respite from the inevitable storms of life. Most importantly, blessings push us into new chapters, through new doors, that are opened before us, whatever they may hold. That is called change, Libby, and it happens whether we want it or not. We grow and change in spite of, and often because of, the influences in our internal and external environments."

Cody was giggling about something, and Norma and Constance were telling her they had to get going. Libby quickly finished her tea. They were right. It was time to go. Norma was talking to Tom on the phone, telling him they were on our way.

Libby now knew about the night with Father Tom, the forbidden love they had shared all these years, to be cut off, albeit temporarily, through Norma's decision to go through with her marriage to Kenny.

So sad, Libby thought, *that Mama would sacrifice her soul mate, in an effort to be good.*

When Libby had shared her sadness about her mom and Tom, Helen had remarked, "There is a season for all things, Libby. While God hates what our terrible decisions do to us, he allows us to be free to choose them. It is the ideal towards which every parent strives, all the while knowing that we are all capable of and indeed do sometimes choose badly. But God's ultimate will includes precious grace, in that while He knew we would choose badly, at times, He would always allow good to come from those bad choices. It is our responsibility to look for the good that will most certainly follow a bad choice. These are the blessings of grace, Libby."

It had been a powerful session. Libby had shared these teachings with her mama and her Gamma.

Most of all, Libby wanted Cody to have a relationship with God, her creator. She wouldn't push her, regarding doctrine, as she didn't believe it was her place to do so. She would expose Cody to all the world's religions, and God would draw her to Himself in His own time and ways.

She knew that Jesus would never force anyone to believe in His teachings, His promise of eternal life. He did just the opposite. He modeled that grace as he gently called people to follow Him, because He offered a path that was easier, in the end, than any we would choose for ourselves.

She had already begun a bedtime ritual with Cody. As she tucked her in each night, Libby would whisper, "Cody, you are wanted, welcomed and worthy. You are good, right, and whole. And you are loved beyond measure. God loves you. I love you. Nana loves you…" She stopped with telling her all the people who loved her because Nana had a similar ritual with Cody, only Nana added the question, "Is that too many people to love you?" They were all careful not to tread on the rituals they were each forming with Cody, like prayers, songs, games, stories, etc. Each of them was carving out their own memories for Cody to cherish.

Libby loved her bedtime ritual with Cody. It was a fun and important one. And it had a tremendous effect on Libby herself. Helen had called that re-parenting oneself. Libby had smiled and said, "Well, it is working." While she felt sorry that her own mother hadn't taught her those things, she was happy that she was doing it with Cody. She also chose to remember how her own mother would lie down with her at night until she was asleep. "She would never let me cry," Libby would remind herself, "at least if she could hear me. She was a good mother in so many ways. I don't want to ever forget that."

Helen had commended her on her desire to focus on the good. "It keeps us sane, as long as we strive to understand the bad, so we can move forward with lessons we have learned."

Helen had taught her, Mama, and Gamma, in one of their conjoint sessions, about our human instinct for self-preservation. Libby knew that Norma had sacrificed her own identity so that she could feel accepted by her mother.

Libby realized that she too had made sacrifices in order to escape her father's abuse.

"Self-preservation can be extremely strong," Helen had told them. "That is because, somewhere deep inside, we know that we are precious, that we are unique, that we are one of a kind. We strive for the ability to acknowledge that truth and remember it when we are being tossed about in the storms of life."

Libby had loved Jerry, but she realized now the kind of love she felt for him wasn't the kind she felt for George Leonard. It was more of an agape love. It was ironic George had saved her life and the life of her unborn daughter. So, in essence, both Jerry and George were important relationships in her life. She refused to hate Jerry and chose to feel gratitude that he came along when he did while simultaneously choosing to be very glad that he was now out of her life. It felt good to be emotionally healthy enough to make that choice.

It had been so healing to see the changes that had taken place in the relationship between Norma and Grandmother. And it touched Libby's heart to see that her mother and Tom still shared a very deep connection, a profound intimacy that most people never find in a lifetime.

Norma came into the kitchen and said, "Libby, we have to go, dear."

Libby asked her to sit down.

"What is it, honey?" Norma's eyes expressed concern as Libby's voice was unusually quiet.

"Mama, Tom coming back when he did, George finding him and saving his life, then finding me and saving our lives. Those were not coincidences." Libby smiled. "They were God-incidents. It's serendipity, don't you think? We're going to be okay, today, Mama, whatever happens! One thing we have all learned is that, despite the only choices we thought we had at the time, even bad ones, God's plans for our lives were not thwarted! I know the sacrifices that both of you made. Tom, for the church before he figured out there was a difference between the church and God. And you, for Grandmother. I can only imagine how hard that must have been for you. But I really do believe that all things work together for good. God has restored what the locusts have eaten, and He will continue to do so."

"Yes, dear daughter. Do you know how precious you are to me?"

Libby laughed and said, "I'm learning. We will continue to do our best. We will continue to make mistakes. Progress not perfection."

"What's important now, Libby, is to move forward to the day care! So you get out there and buckle your child into her car seat!"

Libby laughed and nodded.

As they walked out, Libby recalled a session with Helen. Helen was encouraging her to talk about her relationship with her mother. She had asked Libby, "Do you remember the fourth commandment?" Libby had answered, "Yes, historically, it has not been my favorite." Helen had asked, "Can we talk about why not?"

"Mama, we spent the entire session exploring my misguided attempts to 'honor' my parents. I really want to honor you and Gamma, but in healthy ways, not by sacrificing who I am and what I need. I am so careful sometimes, wanting to say the right things so I don't hurt you or Gamma, but it gets tiring after a while."

Norma replied, "Honey, I think all we get in that rut some-times. We all want this to work. But we are not alone. Holy Spirit is whispering to us all the time. Take care of yourself. Keep yourself healthy, and the rest will follow. I believe that because God loves us all so much. The suffering, either by ourselves, or by the hand of someone else, the suffering is not for naught. God turns it around and brings good from evil every time. Romans 8:28…all things work for good…you taught me that, dear daughter." She hugged her daughter as she let the tears of gratitude flow freely, finally knowing that crying was an important part of healing and knowing that she would not be chastised.

Libby smiled. "Yes, I did, didn't I?"

It felt good to be the teacher. In the school of social work, they had recently been interviewed by the graduate students from the education department. Libby recalled how surprised she was to find out that she had a gift for teaching. She had scored ten out of ten for listening and for teaching what she herself had learned. Her professor had said, "That gift will come in handy as a clinical social worker."

Norma continued, "Okay then, we will honor God by honoring ourselves, by continuing to be the best we can be, by being responsi-ble and accountable for our choices and the actions that follow those choices, and by continuing to discover who we are and what we really want in this journey we call life."

Libby laughed. She knew that Norma was quoting from an arti-cle she had read to her and Gamma at one of their Saturday morn-ing teas. It was written by Oprah Winfrey. She had recently read it herself.

The *O Magazine* was something each of these three generations of women cherished. Helen had recommended it. Libby had sub-scribed to it, and the living room magazine rack was full of the latest issues. That was a miracle all by itself, for Gamma's poker friends to see her living room full of self-help books.

When they got outside, Gamma was chasing Cody around the car, albeit slowly, with her new cane. They walked up to the car when they saw Norma and Libby. Cody was holding on to Gamma's cane. Libby smiled. She looked at her watch. It was 4:30 p.m. The party was supposed to start at 5:00 p.m. and the day care was only ten minutes away, but Libby knew better than to argue with her Gamma and her mother, as both were always very prompt.

"We choose our battles," Libby whispered to herself as she remembered Helen's latest teaching. "Cody Marie, you'd better get in your car seat fast! We have a birfday party to attend."

CHAPTER 9

Rick Browning put the bullets into the chamber of his Glock. He would take it with him, just in case things didn't go as planned. After all, although Kenny and Jerry were alcoholics, they were smart alcoholics and he wasn't taking any chances. And the two druggies? Better to be prepared.

Rick was thinking about Norma and what a very strong and intelligent woman she was. She had stood by Kenny all these years. She had tried her best to help him. He had walked into their kitchen one day and had seen Norma pouring a bottle of vodka down the drain and had called in sick for him on more than one occasion.

Both Kenny and Jerry had attractive wives, who both seemed to care a great deal for them. But they had wanted each other and had actually resented having to keep up appearances by being married and having children and, of course, wait for all the money Norma's mother had to drop into their laps one day.

Rick wondered if Norma had left Kenny because she wanted a relationship with her daughter and granddaughter, minus an alcoholic grandfather.

"Maybe she didn't want her granddaughter growing up the way her daughter had?" He had seen Kenny drunk as a skunk, and it wasn't a pleasant sight.

He knew that Norma's mother was rich. He had, after all, seen the mansion they lived in. But he couldn't put all the pieces together. Originally, the old woman had practically pushed Norma to marry Kenny. Kenny told everyone he had been "handpicked by the old broad." But by the time Kenny was discharged from Window to Your Dreams, he had been overheard telling a coworker, "Hell, I doubt we'll ever see a dime of her money. Norma's mother is a bitch and treats Norma like a dog. Norma takes it though and says she still loves her mother, even though she doesn't like her very much. Can you believe that shit?"

Rick admired the strength of these women. They had pulled together after the birth of Kenny's granddaughter and seemed to be stronger than ever. Rick had always thought Kenny was crazy for not appreciating Norma.

She was as beautiful as she was smart. Rick had actually felt sorry for Kenny when he first found out about him and Jerry. Rick was homophobic and couldn't fathom how Kenny and Jerry could possibly choose each other over Norma and Libby. He was always making fun of them, calling them queers behind their backs. But it had stopped there.

"To each his own," he told his wife. "But now he had photos of me and Jerry? Unacceptable!"

Rick shook his head as if to bring himself back to the present. Well, dear old Kenny can't have his lover or his granddaughter. Nobody treats Rick Browning with disrespect. *He has to pay for the way he humiliated me*, he thought as he put the Glock into the glove box.

What Rick didn't know was that Jerry was right behind him. Rick didn't know that Kenny had convinced Jerry that his daughter was their ticket out of North Carolina and that he was planning to kidnap her from the day care center himself.

Rick pulled up to the alley across from the day care, the alley where the kid was going to be delivered. He was surprised to see that Jerry was pulling up right in front of the center, surprised that their wives were okay with either of them going, but he didn't care.

"Not going to change what has to happen," he said to himself.

Jerry saw Kenny. He was standing across the street with a guy Jerry had never seen before. The stranger was holding a gun to Kenny's back. Jerry almost screamed out loud. While he was trying to decide what to do, Rick got out of his car and headed towards a black sedan.

Jerry said to himself, "This doesn't look good," and he took the Colt 45 out of his glove compartment.

What came next was complete chaos. Rick and the other man argued. Jerry couldn't hear everything they were saying, but it was really heated, something about "the rest of the money."

Then the strange man shot Rick right there in the street. The gun had a silencer on it. He was no amateur. Then another guy appeared from the day care with a little girl. He had his hand over her mouth as she fiercely clung to a backpack.

Jerry shook his head, crying so hard he could hardly see, and just trying to make sense of it all. The strange man who had shot Rick pushed Kenny into the black sedan, leaving Rick lying there in a pool of blood.

Jerry was terrified. "What the hell?" He could hear police sirens. People were running out of the building. Jerry wasn't sure what was happening but figured it had something to do with that little girl. He hadn't seen Cody since she had been born. He had barely glanced at her then, so he had no idea if it was her being kidnapped. Jerry decided, reluctantly, to follow the black sedan. It had Kenny and the kid in the back seat. He had to save Kenny.

Jerry realized he was speeding, but he didn't want to lose the black sedan. He had never driven so fast in his life. They were going so fast Jerry was afraid he would have a wreck and kill himself. He touched the St. Christopher medallion he wore around his neck, a gift from his foster grandmother.

"Protect me, God. Please don't let me die. I want to be better, I promise. But I need help."

It was getting harder and harder to keep up. When they ran a red light, Jerry ran a red light. When they turned onto the interstate, Jerry followed. When they cut over into the turn lane, Jerry followed. Then the black sedan turned off the next exit. They had slowed down some. Jerry was calmer now and realized he had better slow down too, yet keeping them in view.

Where are they going and why? Jerry thought as he turned off the same exit. He hung back, really far this time, because they were the only two cars on the road.

Next thing he knew the black sedan was turning onto a dirt road.

Nothing out here but farms, thought Jerry, getting more and more agitated. He pulled back again because he didn't want to be seen.

He was passing an abandoned farmhouse. Jerry debated whether to pull in behind it or keep going. He couldn't see anything but road in front of him, so he reluctantly pulled over. He waited about fifteen minutes, then started his car, prepared to hunt them down, albeit very slowly.

Then he saw the black sedan coming back. Kenny wasn't in it, but two other guys and the little girl were! Jerry ducked down in his car and waited for them to pass. Then he pulled out from behind the abandoned barn and drove down the road where they had taken Kenny.

He had driven approximately ten minutes when he saw him at the side of a cornfield. He was almost hidden by the corn but had evidently crawled out into the road. He was all bloody. It looked as if he had been shot. Jerry got out of his car and went to him. That's when he realized that Kenny had been shot four times in the chest. He was dead. His pockets turned inside out. They had taken his wallet, all his cash, and his credit cards.

Putting his head into his hands, Jerry wept like a baby. He had really loved Kenny. He was just now realizing how much. Kenny had been everything to him. And now he was gone.

"Why? Why?" Jerry sobbed. "What did he ever do to deserve this? Oh God, my sweet Kenny, my best friend." He wept for a long time. He even thought about taking the gun they had stolen from Norma's mother's house out of his glove compartment and turning it on himself.

Then Jerry panicked, "What if they come back?" He went back to his car and sped away. He couldn't call the police. Suddenly, it dawned upon him. "What if Rick Browning was behind all this?" He recalled the night with him.

It was all Kenny's idea. Kenny was insistent about putting Rick into that compromising situation with Jerry, then insisted about taking photos of them "for leverage," he had said. "Just in case we ever need it."

Jerry hadn't minded very much. He didn't like cheating on Kenny, but it wasn't really cheating because it was what Kenny wanted. So Jerry had done what Kenny had asked. He had sex with a very drunk Rick Browning. He had always thought Rick Browning a handsome man, even if he was a lot older than Jerry was. He had later felt very guilty about it all though because he really loved Kenny. He still felt guilty about it. He wondered why those men killed Rick and why they killed Kenny. He was so scared yet so sad. It had made him sick to leave Kenny lying out there at the side of the road. But he felt he didn't really have a choice. He was a wanted man.

He noticed he was almost out of gas and stopped at the next gas station. It was out in the middle of nowhere, so Jerry felt fairly safe there. It was there, however, that the police caught up with him. They arrested him there, just outside of Hendersonville. They handcuffed him and put him in the squad car.

He could see Libby standing next to the other police car.

"This can't be happening," she was sobbing. "This can't be happening. Please find her. Please find her."

Jerry was astounded. Those strangers, the ones who shot Kenny, they had kidnapped his own daughter. He suddenly felt angry, and he wasn't sure why. It wasn't like he'd ever wanted to know her... until now.

Libby was still talking to the police officer. She had remembered having placed a cell phone in Cody's backpack. The cell phone had a child locator on it. She had given it to Cody for her birthday. She had told the police officer about how excited Cody was to have her own phone, even though she didn't know how to use it yet, for calling anyway.

"She just pushes the buttons, and sometimes a shape or a coloring page will pop up."

She remembered giving Cody the phone. "Looks like you are getting to be a big girl, Cody, and this is to help Mommy keep up with you," she had said. Libby had shown her how she could draw on it as well as listen to her numbers and colors, shapes and alphabet songs as she grew older.

Wow, Jerry thought, *she is a really good mother*. Somehow he knew she would be.

Norma had scared Libby when she started talking about Rick Browning that morning. Libby told the police officer about their conversation and how she had felt silly but still put the cell phone in the zipper compartment of the backpack.

"Just in case," she was telling Sheriff Riley, who commended her for thinking about the tracking device in Cody's backpack. The police knew exactly where to go, thanks to a mother's instincts.

"Better not to take chances," she had told herself when she slipped it into the backpack. "You are getting paranoid, Libby. Seen too many *Law and Order* shows." She had laughed to herself. "Time for some romance novels."

Cody had squealed with delight when she got the giraffe backpack. Giraffes were her favorite animal since their trip to the Asheville zoo.

Jerry was still sitting in the back of the police car. Libby was still standing outside with a female police officer, who was holding her gently as she cried. She then leaned over and whispered something into her ear. Libby looked up and started running toward a third police car that had just pulled up.

Libby grabbed the little girl, his daughter, and was thanking the police officer for her help. Jerry craned his neck this time to get a good look at his kid. *She's a cute kid*, he thought, surprised that he even cared, one way or the other. *Looks like Libby.*

Cody felt limp in Libby's arms. "Exhausted and scared to death," Libby said. She was told they found Cody on the side of the road. From what Libby could surmise, whoever kidnapped her had decided to let her go. "My poor baby," Libby was saying. "My baby."

"Well, they didn't just let her go," Sheriff Riley said. "They pushed her out of the car. She's a little bloody and bruised, but I think she's going to be okay."

Just then the black sedan came speeding by, followed by another police car. They were shooting at each other. The police officers shot a tire out, and the car came to a screeching halt. The men in the car were quarreling. The younger guy shot his partner, then turned the gun on himself.

"Oh no, you don't," said Officer Riley as he smashed in the window and took the gun from the stranger's hand. "You, my friend, are going to tell us what all this craziness has been about."

As fate would have it, the stranger who had been shot was a well-known drug dealer and wanted in three states. The younger guy was his accomplice and had some minor drug use charges but no charges for trying to sell. He was on parole. He was offering to be a state's witness and was now willing to tell the officers what happened.

He had been a witness to Rick Browning's murder and to the kidnapping. He told them all about Rick Browning's plan to "kidnap Cody and then kill Kenny, but Sam killed Browning first."

Jerry heard the name and smiled. "Cody is her name."

Rick had been waiting for them "around the corner from the day care," Jerry heard the stranger saying. The stranger had "gone in to use the john and had come right back out."

The guy who had taken his daughter was probably going to get a lighter sentence because he was willing to testify. Jerry was incensed. One of them had killed Kenny. The other had driven the car. He hated them both.

His partner and Mr. Browning had "quarreled over the money Mr. Browning was supposed to bring with him but hadn't." Mr. Browning was too concerned about Kenny Vault, who was already in the back seat when Sam had returned with the kid. They were shouting at each other. Rick had turned around then because Sam had grabbed him by the neck and told him he "wanted his money and wanted it now." Rick had laughed and said, "I didn't bring it with me. I'll have to get it to you later."

When the other kidnapper, Sam, realized he wasn't going to pay them any more money, he shot Mr. Browning, took his credit cards and cash, and left him lying there in a pool of blood. They had then driven out to the abandoned barn.

Jerry listened as the guy spilled his guts. He had remembered traveling down that old road years before with his biological father. He also knew that the younger guy was lying. He had seen it all.

Maybe they'll listen to me and give me a break, he thought. *At least they won't know which of us is lying. It will cast some doubt on what that SOB is saying.*

"It wasn't the older guy that shot Rick Browning," Jerry shouted to Sheriff Riley. "It was him. He's lying through his teeth. I saw the whole thing."

"You're the one who's lying. Your word against mine," the witness shouted back.

Jerry started to get out of the police car, but Sheriff Riley pushed him back in. "We'll sort it all out later, but you aren't going anywhere, mister." Riley wondered why Jerry had been crying. His face was red and puffy. It was obvious he had been crying for quite some time and wondered if he might be telling the truth about Kenny Vault being his lover.

"We'll see what happened, buddy. We found the Glock in Sam's car, but we know it's not the gun used to kill the Galyon housekeeper, Maria, so you are still a prime suspect there."

The witness continued his testimony while Jerry sat there and cried some more.

"Sam told me we could get rid of Kenny too, but not there."

"We'll take him down to where those cornfields are. We'll shoot him there," Sam had said, "and then we'll hide him in a cornfield."

"I didn't want to kill anyone. Honest, I didn't. But once we were there, Sam had shot Kenny four times in the chest. I'm telling you the truth. It was Sam."

It really bothered Jerry that this young punk was lying. It's one thing to stretch the truth, which is what he had done, or so he thought. But this guy was out-and-out lying. He just knew it!

"He killed Kenny. And he took my daughter," Jerry cried.

"We'll see," said the police officer who was in the car with Jerry. He actually believed Jerry. "But if you're telling the truth, I'd say he's wiped those prints off and disposed of the gun."

186

"What will happen to me?" Jerry was sobbing. "They killed my partner. Kenny was my partner. I loved him with all my heart. He was here to attend his granddaughter's birthday party. I was coming to the party as well. Then, whoosh, they had killed Mr. Browning, taken Cody, pushed Kenny into their car, and sped off. I was following them because I wanted to protect my partner and my daughter!" Jerry was sobbing. He was partially telling the truth, but would they believe him?

"We'll use your testimony, if it turns out to be true, to clear all of this up. And if needed, we'll place you in the witness protection program," Sheriff Riley was telling the stranger. "But if you so much as smoke a joint, we'll know it," he hissed as the stranger was handcuffed and put into the back of the other police car. "And if you're lying, you are going away for a very long time."

Jerry turned around to get another look at Cody, but they were gone.

It had all happened so quickly, Libby's head was spinning. They had all watched Cody blow out her candle, eat cake, and open presents. She had squealed with delight at each and every one of them.

After opening the last gift, Cody had turned to her friends and had given each of them a party toy to take home with them. Then she had compassionately placed her new toys into the arms of her friends who had no gifts to open "so we can all play together," she had said.

She was so kind and affectionate and always thinking of others. Norma and Libby had looked at each other when she shared her toys and laughed simultaneously.

"The apple doesn't fall far from the tree, does it, my dear?" Norma had said.

"No, it doesn't." Libby had laughed in agreement.

"Christian agape love?" they said and laughed in unison.

Libby was very proud of her daughter for caring about the feelings of her classmates. She didn't want them to feel left out. Libby had been the same way growing up, always making sure that her friends were included.

A healthy trait, Libby had thought. But she had made a mental note about it. She wanted to ask Helen how one could tell the difference between being giving and selfless as a Christian and being codependent.

Cody had toddled over to the door to get her backpack to show her friends. Libby had gotten up to retrieve her. The door opened, and Cody was grabbed before Libby could do anything but scream. She ran down the hallway and out into the street hoping to catch them, but Cody was gone, along with her giraffe backpack.

Libby dialed 911, then sat down on the curb, crying hysterically.

George followed her out. She was beside herself with grief. He gently picked her up and carried her to his car, shouting to Norma and Tom that he was taking her home to rest. He said he wanted to "give Libby a chance to rest in case the police needed to talk to her again."

"We will place a man outside of your house, just in case," the sheriff said kindly. "Take her on home."

Norma had also called 911. The police officers had responded quickly, questioning the staff and the parents. It all happened so fast. Nobody, not one single person, could give them a description.

"All I saw was an arm," one of the parents had said tearfully. "The door opened. She was grabbed. She was gone."

Constance Galyon had fainted right in the middle of the street. The sheriff asked Norma and Tom if they wanted to take her to the ER. He had called an ambulance. They nodded, both of them numb. They got in their car and followed the ambulance to Transylvania Hospital.

Norma was worried about her mother's blood pressure. She was afraid she might have had a stroke. When they arrived at the ER, they had given Grandmother a shot of Ativan. There was no evidence of a stroke.

"She's just overwrought," the ambulance attendant had said. "She was crying for her granddaughter, but she should be okay now."

And she was. When they were sure it was a panic attack and not a stroke, they sent her home.

At home, Gamma was resting in her bed upstairs. Cody was sitting on the floor, playing with her new toys. She looked really tired and weak, but George attributed it to the kidnapping. Tom, George, Libby, and Norma were all still talking to the police officer who had followed them home, trying to remember facts, telling the police officers what they knew about Kenny and Jerry and about Rick Browning. Norma told them about Kenny and Jerry being fired. She told them about the photos she had found in Kenny's desk drawer.

"We checked on the black sedan," said Officer Riley. "It wasn't registered to Jerry or the two guys who kidnapped Cody. Probably stolen." Then he said to George, "It's a good thing your wife remembered the giraffe. Try to get some rest. We'll talk again tomorrow."

As he was walking out the door, Libby suddenly remembered that it was Cody who had grabbed the backpack as she was yanked out the door. "It was a birthday present. She was really excited to get it…" Her voice trailed off into a whisper. She felt like she was going to faint herself.

Pick up at George was insistent. "Yes, officer, she needs to rest."

The officer nodded in agreement as George let Libby upstairs to her bedroom. He took her shoes off, gave her a sedative, and pulled the covers up under her chin. "Sleep for a minute, my darling. You need your strength for Cody. You know how much energy that child has. I'll bring her up to take a nap with you."

Libby smiled and agreed to lie down. "I love you," she said as he tucked her in. "Bring her up soon."

George was barely holding his own grief in check. He loved Cody, and he already thought of her as his own daughter. He wiped the tears from his own eyes and went back downstairs to see if the other officer needed him any further. She hadn't, so he took Cody in his arms and held her close to his heart.

"You're going to be okay, sweetheart. I promise you that." He didn't realize he had started crying again, until Cody reached up and wiped a tear off his cheek.

CHAPTER 10

George was afraid to put Cody in bed, even though she was nodding off. Being a physician, he wondered how badly she had been injured when she was pushed out of the car. He had seen the bruises and the blood on her dress earlier.

She could have been thrown out while the car was still moving, George thought.

But he didn't want to alarm Libby. Cody wanted to play with her new toys, and they needed to talk to the police officers. It was hard for Libby to go to bed without Cody, but she had agreed since Cody was so enamored with her birthday gifts.

He decided to examine Cody more closely. Looking at her now, he surmised that she had obviously been thrown from a moving car or perhaps even worse. She was limp and listless in his arms. George was crying and telling Cody, "Honey, you have to stay awake. We're going to take you to the hospital where the nice doctors are going to help you feel better."

He couldn't believe he didn't have his medical bag with him. He had taken it into the day care because one of Cody's little classmates had taken the teacher's purse off her desk and had cut his finger on a razor blade she had in there. Everyone had been fussing over Cody, watching her open her presents. The boy had been swift, before anyone could stop him. George had told them not to be alarmed. He was a doctor. He had gone out to his car and gotten his bag so he could clean the wound and stitch it up, if necessary. The boy was fine.

But Cody is not fine, he thought. He was worried about the bleeding, which had gone unnoticed until he took her coat off. "God, please let me get my baby girl to the hospital in time." He was remembering his deceased wife now and their unborn child. *Not again*, he thought. *Please, not again. God, I beg you. Let this child live.*

"It's at the day care," George said out loud. He had been so worried about Cody and Libby, whom he had followed out into the street, he had left the bag in the day care center and hadn't even given it a second thought. "You're a doctor, you fool. How could you have been so careless?" Part of him was beating himself up something terrible. Another part reminded him that God was in charge. His will would be done for reasons he might never understand until he passed on himself. "Okay, just breathe," he said to himself. "Time is of the essence."

Cody began to throw up, just a little at first but then more and more, and she was holding her side. "Hurts daddy," Cody said.

George's heart missed a beat. She had called him daddy. And now she was going limp in his arms. He handed Cody to Tom and quickly called the hospital.

"Meet me at the ER door," he was telling his colleague.

Cody kept drifting off to sleep.

"Stay awake, sweetheart, stay awake." George asked Tom and Norma to go with him to the hospital. "I need you to hold her and keep her awake, Norma. There's something bad going on with her. I think it might be her spleen." George was pretty sure it was. "What if they kicked her? What if she's hemorrhaging? Check on Libby, Norma, then get to the car."

Tom grabbed their coats and headed to the car with Cody. He felt resolved right then and there that Cody was going to be okay. He had a peace about it all, a peace that even surprised him. Norma grabbed the woolen Native American blanket that had protected her from the cold when she was born and wrapped it around her.

When they got to the ER, as if for a sense of confirmation, George told Cody, "You are going to be okay. But the doctor will make you all better."

"Daddy a doctor," Cody had whispered again as they took her back to examine her.

Again, George's heart had skipped a beat. "My baby," he wept. "Please don't take another one from me. God, help me to trust you always."

"Apparently, Cody fell on something sharp, and it ruptured her spleen," George's colleague came out, shaking his head. "She's lost a lot of blood. We need to give her a transfusing. She's type A."

Libby's blood type was O, as was Norma's. George was O as well.

Norma started crying as she told George, "Kenny is type A, and he's dead. Or Jerry, and God only knows where he is right now."

Tom overheard. "I'm type A." Tom had gotten up and gone to her. "Take me back now and let me give you whatever you need."

George's colleague was quick to answer. "Let's go then."

Tom followed him down the hall.

While Tom was donating blood for Cody, Norma was having an awakening.

"Coincidence? Maybe, but doubtful." Norma thought back to the night before she married Kenny. It was the only time she had been with Tom. "Is it possible that Tom is Libby's real father and Cody's grandfather?" She could hardly contain her excitement. But at the same time, she was deathly afraid that Cody might not make it.

Little did she know that Tom was now wondering the same thing. *Cody does have my blond curly hair*, he thought. I don't know why I didn't see it before. He guessed it was because Libby's hair was also blond. *But not curly.* Tom was now smiling to himself.

"God works in mysterious ways." He looked up, as if conversing with the Almighty. "And he had an odd sense of timing sometimes, at least odd to us mere mortals."

He was more than pleased. Not only did God bring him back to his beloved Norma, but he had given him a daughter and a grand-daughter. Now he knew Cody was going to be all right. And now, so did Norma.

Norma had excused herself and gone to the chapel.

"Dear God," she prayed. "I don't even know why I am here. I know that you are going to spare our little Cody, and I thank you for that. I guess I am here to try and figure all of this out, but I have a feeling I will never really understand the wonder of Your love. So I am not even going to question it. I am just going to be grateful. Do you think that odd of me?" She had laughed out loud because she had a history of being a worrier like her mother. "From the very pits of evil you brought love. Please help me to trust you always."

She hadn't realized she was praying out loud and that Tom had later come to the chapel as well. He leaned over the pew and touched her shoulders. Then he climbed over the pew like a little boy. He held her, kissed her, and told her how much she meant to him.

Tom tilted her chin up and said, "She's our granddaughter, Norma. We consummated our love and made a baby who was destined to grow up and give us a grandbaby. I know it's true, Norma." He was smiling profusely, acting like a kid who had just received a lifetime supply of candy. She knew for certain that God had given them both a second chance for a lifetime of love. Now they would wait for Cody to recover. Tom told Norma that he had come to love Libby as his own daughter and Cody as a granddaughter. "And come to find out, Libby is my biological daughter and Cody my true-blood granddaughter." He laughed with the joy of a child.

Norma laughed too. His joy was contagious.

Then he got serious, took Norma's hand in his, and started praying.

"Our loving creator God," he prayed, "we know that your love for Cody and your plans for her life are far greater than anything we could possibly imagine. We ask for patience right now so that we can wait for your healing hand to touch her and heal her. And, God, thank you. Thank you that you are using my blood to do that."

Norma had opened her eyes and smiled at him.

Then he prayed the Lord's Prayer, and Norma joined in softly as they still had their hands clasped together.

The surgeon walked in just as they had finished praying. Cody was responding well to the transfusion. They had stopped the bleeding, repaired her spleen, and she was going to be just fine. They walked back to the waiting room together.

Tom and Norma hugged George and Libby silently. No one said a word. There were no words sufficient enough to express the gratitude they were all feeling. It was enough just to hold each other and rejoice in the bright ending to a very difficult day.

Norma thought of the movie she and Tom had watched the night before and smiled. They had a whole lifetime still ahead of them. Today was fading fast into the night, but as Scarlett O'Hara had so amply put it, "Tomorrow is another day."

EPILOGUE

At Cody's fifth birthday party, George patted Libby's growing belly and said lovingly, "Okay, Cody Leonard, your baby brother just told me to tell you happy birthday and to remind you to make your wish and blow out your candles."

Cody laughed and said, "Mommy's cake will be chocolate, and I'll get lots of presents."

Everyone laughed. Libby touched her mother's hand, whose hand was resting on Gamma's hand, whose hand was resting on Cody's shoulder.

It was a memorable moment. Grandmother was now "Gamma" to anyone who addressed her. She said it suited her and was happy that her worrisome side was slowly melting away.

Libby and George had been married almost four years. George had adopted Cody right away with Libby's blessing. Jerry was safely behind bars and was no longer a threat to them or to Cody.

Norma and Tom had recently celebrated their third anniversary. They also had decided to make a permanent move into Galyon mansion in Cashiers. Constance was not as spry as she used to be. She was in a wheelchair now, recovering from hip replacement.

Gamma had been grateful that Tom and Norma wanted to "take care of her in her old age." While hating that she had robbed herself of so much because of her obsession with status, she realized that the sacrifices she had made for all the worthwhile charities in the community were being graciously returned to her tenfold and she whispered a prayer of Thanksgiving in her heart.

Libby had welcomed Tom as her biological father with an open and thankful heart. Tom was very supportive and protective of her. Initially, they had grieved together all the lost years. They both had finally decided, however, not to let the past rob them of a promising future, and it hadn't.

George and Libby had wanted to get married right away, and Tom and Norma had patiently waited for their own ceremony. Just a few weeks after George and Libby's wedding, Tom had fallen on an icy driveway and had to be hospitalized for three months. After that, he had intensive physical and occupational therapy. It had been tragic the way he had fractured his back, all the way from L-3 to S-1. He had also broken an arm and a leg. But Norma knew he would be okay.

"God wanted us together all those years ago," Norma had told her mother. "He would not let us down now."

And he hadn't. But it had been hard on them, a true test of faith in challenges they never dreamed they would face.

Norma had taken very good care of him and had not cared one bit what people were surely saying about his living there in her home when they were not yet married. Norma had been thrilled when her own mother had suggested it.

"We will just have him move in here," she had said. "He certainly can't take care of himself now, can he?"

Constance Galyon was being transformed, as were Libby and Norma. Connie was fond of reminding her friends that "true Christians don't care what others think about them. They simply do what God calls them to do, even if it looks bad to others who, in their ignorance, don't know any better."

George had been very pleased when Libby had gotten pregnant. They were so happy to become husband and wife that they hadn't even thought about planning any further other than their wedding. Cody had been their flower girl; and Maria's nephew, Carlos, had been their ring bearer. Those two were very close, best friends in fact!

Since Maria's death they had made a decision to stay in touch with their dear housekeeper's family, and they had.

"Maria would have been so pleased to see Carlos as our ring bearer," Libby had told her mother.

Norma had agreed.

George had been so nervous the night of his marriage to Libby, he marveled even to this very day that they were married at all. His practice was booming, and having been called in for an emergency the morning of his wedding, he had almost missed it.

When he had finally gotten to the church, he realized he had forgotten the ring. It was a beautiful platinum with brilliant diamond baguettes on each side to match the solitaire he had given her when he proposed. Libby hadn't minded at all. She just wanted to be his wife, and the ring would have to wait. Her tendencies toward perfectionism were melting away.

Libby was so happy that night. They had waited until their wedding night to make love. Libby had been pleased that George suggested it, knowing all she had suffered in her life, thus far.

They had slept together for almost a month before their wedding, but that is all they had done. He hadn't even touched her breasts, even though he feared he would go mad just thinking about it.

Libby had just needed George to hold her. They cuddled every night and enjoyed pillow talk (something Libby had read about and she and Helen had discussed but until now Libby had never experienced). Because of her history, George had understood her need for it and really enjoyed himself.

Talking until wee hours of the night were actually quite satisfying—emotionally, that is. Physically, it was difficult. All he could think about that entire month, he confessed later, was wanting to "ravish your body." Libby had never felt so cherished, and George was ecstatic.

George knew Libby had not had a satisfying sexual experience at all up to that point, certainly not with her father and certainly not with Jerry. She had confided in him about the sex feeling good physically with her father, which made her feel ashamed emotionally and mentally. She had been a wreck, wishing she was dead on more days than not.

She had never felt any pleasure with Jerry. "He was not interested in romantic tenderness," Libby had told him. "It was just sex, quick and simple." Libby had been so disappointed when she realized that Jerry wasn't interested in whether she was pleased or not, as long as he had been satisfied.

Even on their wedding night, George had held her gently for what seemed like an eternity. He had wanted her to be sure she was ready. Libby had been the one to initiate their lovemaking. She was "more than ready," she had told him after he had held her and gently touched her for almost a solid hour.

She had compared themselves to Adam and Eve. "I am making love for the first time in my life," she confided in him. "I can't get enough of you, Dr. Leonard," she had said lovingly.

"And I can't get enough of you, Libby Leonard," he replied.

She had rubbed his head, rubbed his back, then rubbed his chest. She knew he was "crazy mad" about her. He had said it often enough. And so she wanted to make him "crazy mad" for her sexually.

She had slowly moved her hands from his feet all the way up to his face. She had been surprised that he was ready for her. "You have waited a long time, haven't you, my love?" Libby had tears in her eyes when she whispered in his ear. "You won't be sorry you waited for me, Dr. Leonard."

Then George, having been given Libby's blessing, had hungrily explored her body, from the top of her head to the tips of her toes. He caressed her a long time. Libby moaned with pleasure as he touched her. She was hungry for their bodies to unite in that way, God's intended way. Two becoming one flesh. Two individuals becoming one relationship.

She told him to keep his eyes open. "I want to look at you, my love. I want to keep reminding myself that it is you inside me, your face, your body, loving me, really loving me."

He had opened his eyes and smiled at her. He kissed her like he had never kissed her before.

They had both been hurt, but God had not forsaken them. In fact, He had given them the gift of a life covenant, a precious daughter and a son on the way.

Cody grew into a beautiful young woman. She and Maria's son, Carlos, were the best of friends. He had confided to his mother that he was going to marry Cody one day. She had not said a word to Libby, or to Carlos, but she had seen Cody kissing a young man just the other day, outside the soup kitchen, where she dropped off vegetables and fruits.

Cody was almost eighteen and had met a man who "makes me melt just looking at him," she had breathlessly shared with her mother.

"You're all going to meet him at my graduation," she had said sweetly at one of the Saturday teas the four of them still cherished.

"I know you are going to like him. I met him at the soup kitchen. He volunteers there on Fridays, just like I do. We've only known each other a few weeks, but I know he's the one. He works four days a week from home, but says the soup kitchen comes before anything else on Fridays. You would never know it by the way he dresses or the car he drives, but he is quite wealthy," Libby had told Gamma.

Gamma had been pleased, not so much because he was wealthy, but because Libby's description of him and how they met reminded her of her dear Hugo.

"The manager at the soup kitchen told me that he is rich, but he doesn't let his money go to his head," Libby proclaimed. "It was all true, Gamma. I checked him out, just like you checked Grandfather Hugo out all those years ago. He has a level head on his shoulders and insists on being at the food kitchen every Friday, albeit to his mother's dismay. She gets angry at him for not taking a big interest in the family business as his father does. It's a big business too, Gamma, a conglomerate, really. His late grandfather, Rick Browning, started their huge time-share company called Window to Your Dreams."

Only the beginning…

INDIVIDUAL AND SMALL-GROUP DISCUSSION QUESTIONS

1.
    a. Which character(s) did you identify with the most in the beginning?
    b. Why?
    c. What about toward the end? Same character or another? Why?

2.
    a. We all have one basic need, and this is to love and be loved. All our other needs spring from this very basic human desire.
    b. Do you feel loved?
    c. Why or why not?

3.
    a. Which of your unmet needs screamed or whispered as you read this novel?
    b. List in importance the top two needs and answer the question: "Why are these needs important to me?" Do

you have a better sense of how to get those needs met now?

4.

    a.   Did they have two or more parts of yourself in conflict? What was the conflict about?

    b.   Which part won the conflict and why?

5.

    a.   Which part is your priority now that you've finished the book?

    b.   Is it in the same spot of priority now, or has it moved since reading the novel?

6.   Have you ever been confused about the differences between codependency and the Christian virtue of martyrdom? Did the book help clarify some of the confusion?

7.

    a.   When have you chosen to love, forgive, and focus on the good?

    b.   Did that choice work out well for you? Why or why not?

8.   Are you in a relationship that is unhealthy for you? If yes, why do you stay?

9.   What does the term *hitting bottom* mean to you?

10. Have you ever been in the position of loving someone, giving all you had to give, and not being appreciated or even thanked?

11. Have you ever felt empty, void of feeling, and unable to give any more of yourself to anyone, least of all yourself?

12. With more clarity and direction, are you ready to be unflinching about life's pain so you never give up hope about the possibilities that still remain?

13. Just as the characters in this story, we are all in the process of transformation! It is important to grieve what might have been and it is equally important to turn the page in the next chapter of your life! Are you ready? If no, how will you know when you are ready?

14. Did reading the novel help you to include yourself in your circle of care?

15. If yes, discuss which character and/or which section/chapter was the one that moved you closer to turning the page into a new chapter of your life's journey.

16.
   a. What if Constance had not as worried about her status in the community as she was about what she believed was God's call to keep her community's alive?
   b. Does it matter which answer is true?
   c. Why or why not?

17.

    a. Have you ever given everything you had and then some, not for attention or to be liked but just because you wanted to help someone in need and you didn't receive so much as a thank you or even an acknowledgement?

    b. How did that make you feel?

    c. Were you able to use it as a steppingstone into a better chapter? Can you now, if you didn't before?

    d. How did you move past it?

Bless you for choosing to read a novel that was entertaining as well as clinical in nature. Please let me know if you enjoyed the book and let me know if you would like to see the second novel in the trilogy!

Sincerely,
Angie Galler Bowen, LCSW, CCBT

ABOUT THE AUTHOR

Angie earned her master's in clinical social work at University of Tennessee. She has held licenses in Tennessee and Florida and currently maintains a license in North Carolina.

Certified in cognitive behavioral therapy and rational hypnotherapy, Angie has extensive training and expertise in helping people who struggle with depression, anxiety, forgiveness, obsessive-compulsive, and perfectionistic behaviors when trying to maintain healthy relationships.

With twenty-five years of clinical private practice, fifteen years facilitating social skills workshops and retreats, and a background of serving as adjunct professor of psychology, social work, and social welfare, Angie was blessed to also conduct continuing education workshops for the University of Tennessee and National Association of Cognitive Behavioral Therapy.

She enjoyed appearing on local TV and radio to promote individual peace during holidays. She has served as EAP counselor for Florida military and USPS and conducted grief groups for children in public schools.

Angie lost her husband to cancer in 2018. He was her greatest supporter during the writing of *Saints Codependent*. It is her hope that while deeply entertaining as a novel, this book continues to direct a purposeful focus toward our ability to overcome physical, psychological, social, and spiritual stumbling blocks to healthy relationships. This is her deepest desire as a woman and clinician.

Now retired, Angie's favorite pastime is spending time with her grandchildren and her new puppy, Georgia. You can reach her at angiegallerbowenlcsw@yahoo.com. I hope that was entertaining and provided helpful clinical insights that are crucial to relationship skill building and maintenance.